D1481370

TABLE OF CONTENTS

Copyright © Mometrix Media. You have been licensed one copy of this document for personal use only. Any other reproduction or redistribution is strictly prohibited. All rights reserved.

Top 20 Test Taking Tips

1. Carefully follow all the test registration procedures
2. Know the test directions, duration, topics, question types, how many questions
3. Setup a flexible study schedule at least 3-4 weeks before test day
4. Study during the time of day you are most alert, relaxed, and stress free
5. Maximize your learning style; visual learner use visual study aids, auditory learner use auditory study aids
6. Focus on your weakest knowledge base
7. Find a study partner to review with and help clarify questions
8. Practice, practice, practice
9. Get a good night's sleep; don't try to cram the night before the test
10. Eat a well balanced meal
11. Know the exact physical location of the testing site; drive the route to the site prior to test day
12. Bring a set of ear plugs; the testing center could be noisy
13. Wear comfortable, loose fitting, layered clothing to the testing center; prepare for it to be either cold or hot during the test
14. Bring at least 2 current forms of ID to the testing center
15. Arrive to the test early; be prepared to wait and be patient
16. Eliminate the obviously wrong answer choices, then guess the first remaining choice
17. Pace yourself; don't rush, but keep working and move on if you get stuck
18. Maintain a positive attitude even if the test is going poorly
19. Keep your first answer unless you are positive it is wrong
20. Check your work, don't make a careless mistake

Copyright © Mometrix Media. You have been licensed one copy of this document for personal use only. Any other reproduction or redistribution is strictly prohibited. All rights reserved.

Mechanics

Vectors

Vectors are mathematical quantities with both magnitude and direction. A vector is most commonly described by the magnitude of its components in the relevant coordinate system. Vectors may exist in any number of dimensions, but for applications in mechanics they will most often be in either two or three. A vector is generally denoted by a letter either in boldface type or with an arrow above it.

Adding or subtracting vectors is as simple as adding or subtracting their components. For instance, given the two vectors a = <1,5,7> and b = <5,-3,3>, $a + b$ = <(1+5),(5-3),(7+3)> = <6,2,10>. If vectors are given as a length and an angle, it may be necessary to use trigonometry to convert these to orthogonal components.

Visually, adding a vector is accomplished by drawing the second vector starting from the endpoint of the first vector. To visually subtract a vector, draw both vectors starting from the origin. The difference will be the vector from the endpoint of the second to the endpoint of the first.

Vector addition has many of the same relevant properties as scalar addition. It is commutative, in that $a + b = b + a$, and associative, in that $(a + b) + c = a + (b + c)$.

There are a few different ways to multiply vectors, though none of them is exactly the same as algebraic multiplication. For instance, one way to multiply vectors is to multiply a vector by a scalar. If we are to multiply vector a by scalar s, we can only multiply the magnitude of a by the absolute value of s. The direction of the product will be the same as a so long as s is positive; if s is negative, the resulting vector will be in the opposite direction. To divide by s, we would simply multiply a by 1/s. One common example of this kind of operation in physics is in the equation for force. To find force, we multiply mass (scalar) by acceleration (vector). Of course, since mass will always be positive, the direction of the resulting vector (force) will always be in the direction of the acceleration.

<u>Cross products</u>
When two vectors are being multiplied for a vector product ($a \times b = c$), the equation will be written $c = ab \sin \varphi$, where φ is the smaller of the two angles between a and b. Because in this form the multiplication of a and b is indicated with the ×, this resulting vector is often known as the cross product. Of course, if a and b are parallel, then $a \times b = 0$. The direction of c will be perpendicular to the plane that contains both a and b by the right-hand rule. It should be noted that the commutative law does not apply to this kind of multiplication. Instead, we may say that the cross product is an anticommutative function, meaning that $b \times a = -a \times b$. This kind of equation will be used in the formula for torque.

An alternative method for calculating the cross product is to take the determinant of a 3x3 matrix composed of the two vectors along with the unit vectors i, j, and k. For vectors a = <2,3,6>, b = <1,1,4>:

Copyright © Mometrix Media. You have been licensed one copy of this document for personal use only. Any other reproduction or redistribution is strictly prohibited. All rights reserved.

$$a \times b = \begin{vmatrix} i & j & k \\ 2 & 3 & 6 \\ 1 & 1 & 4 \end{vmatrix} = i(12-6) + j(6-8) + k(2-3)$$

So **a** x **b** = 6**i** – 2**j** – **k**. Conversely, **b** x **a** = -6**i** + 2**j** + **k**.

<u>Dot products</u>
There are two different methods for multiplying two vectors: one way yields a vector product, and one way yields a scalar product. If we take the vectors **a** and **b** and decide to solve for a scalar product, we will set up this equation: $\mathbf{a} \cdot \mathbf{b} = ab \cos \varphi$. In this equation, a is the magnitude of the vector **a**, b is the magnitude of the vector **b**, and φ is the angle between **a** and **b**. Another way to arrive at the same scalar product is to multiply each component of one vector by the corresponding component in the other vector and sum the results: $\mathbf{a} \cdot \mathbf{b} = a_x b_x + a_y b_y + a_z b_z$. Since there are only scalars on the right side of the equation, the resulting product will be a scalar. This product is often referred to as a dot product, since the left side of the equation is often written with the expression, "$\mathbf{a} \cdot \mathbf{b}$" (a dot b). This kind of equation is exemplified by the formula for work, in which a scalar (work) is found by multiplying two vectors (force and displacement).

<u>Displacement</u>
When something changes its location from one place to another, it is said to have undergone *displacement*. If we can determine the original and final position of the object, then we can determine the total displacement with this simple equation: *Δx = final position – original position*. If the object has moved in the positive direction, then the final position will be greater than the original position, so we can say that the change was positive. If the final position is less than the original, however, displacement will be negative. Displacement along a straight line is a very simple example of a vector quantity: that is, it has both a magnitude and a direction. If an object travels from position x = -5 cm to x = 5 cm, it has undergone a displacement of 10 cm. If it traverses the same path in the opposite direction, its displacement is -10 cm. A vector that spans the object's displacement in the direction of travel is known as a displacement vector, with units of length.

<u>Determining Position</u>
In order to determine anything about the motion of an object, we must first locate it. In other words, we must be able to describe its position relative to some reference point, often called an *origin*. If we consider the origin as the zero point of an axis, then the positive direction of the axis will be the direction in which measuring numbers are getting larger, and the negative direction is that in which the numbers are getting smaller. If a particle is located 5 cm from the origin in the positive direction of the x-axis, its location is said to be x = 5 cm. If another particle is 5 cm from the origin in the negative direction of the x-axis, its position is x = -5 cm. These two particles are 10 cm apart. A vector whose starting point is the origin and whose endpoint is the location of an object is that object's position vector, with units of length.

Velocity

<u>Instantaneous velocity</u>
There are two types of velocity that are commonly considered in physics: average velocity and instantaneous velocity. In order to obtain the *instantaneous velocity* of an object, we must find its average velocity and then try to decrease Δt as close as possible to zero. As Δt decreases, it approaches what is known as a *limiting value*, bringing the average velocity very close to the

- 6 -

Copyright © Mometrix Media. You have been licensed one copy of this document for personal use only. Any other reproduction or redistribution is strictly prohibited. All rights reserved.

instantaneous velocity. Instantaneous velocity is most easily discussed in the context of calculus-based physics.

Average velocity

There are two types of velocity that are commonly considered in physics: average velocity and instantaneous velocity. If we want to calculate the *average velocity* of an object, we must know two things. First, we must know its displacement, or the distance it has covered. Second, we must know the time it took to cover this distance. Once we have this information, the formula for average velocity is quite simple: $v_{av} = (x_f - x_i)/(t_f - t_i)$, where the subscripts i and f denote the initial and final values of the position and time. In other words, the average velocity is equal to the change in position divided by the change in time. This calculation will indicate the average distance that was covered per unit of time. Average velocity is a vector and will always point in the same direction as the displacement vector (since time is a scalar and always positive).

Kinematic equations

The phenomenon of constant acceleration allows physicists to construct a number of helpful equations. Perhaps the most fundamental equation of an object's motion is the position equation: $x = at^2/2 + v_it + x_i$. If the object is starting from rest at the origin, this equation reduces to $x = at^2/2$. The position equation can be rearranged to give the displacement equation: $\Delta x = at^2/2 + v_it$. If the object's acceleration is unknown, the position or displacement may be found by the equation $\Delta x = (v_f + v_i)t/2$. If the position of an object is unknown, the velocity may be found by the equation $v = v_i + at$. Similarly, if the time is unknown, the velocity after a given displacement may be found by the equation $v = sqrt(v_i^2 + 2a\Delta x)$.

Acceleration

Acceleration is the change in the velocity of an object. Like velocity, acceleration may be computed as an average or an instantaneous quantity. To calculate average acceleration, we may use this simple equation: $a_{av} = (v_f - v_i)/(t_f - t_i)$, where the subscripts i and f denote the initial and final values of the velocity and time. The so-called instantaneous acceleration of an object can be found by reducing the time component to the limiting value until instantaneous velocity is approached. Acceleration will be expressed in units of distance divided by time squared; for instance, meters per second squared. Like position and velocity, acceleration is a vector quantity and will therefore have both magnitude and direction.

Projectile motion

When we discuss *projectile motion*, we are referring to the movement of an object through two dimensions during a free fall. Two-dimensional motion may be described using the same equations as one-dimensional motion, but two equations must be considered simultaneously. While setting up some basic equations for projectile motion, we will assume that the rate of acceleration towards the ground is g = 9.8 m/s, and that the effect of air resistance can be ignored. If a projectile is launched under such ideal conditions, we may say that its initial velocity is $v_0 = v_0cos(\theta)i + v_0sin(\theta)j$. These two velocity components are sometimes written as v_{x0} and v_{y0}, respectively.

Example: If a cannon located at a height of 5 m above ground level fires a cannonball 250 m/s at an angle of pi/6 from the horizontal, how far will the cannonball travel before hitting the ground?

When the cannonball hits the ground, it has been displaced by -5 m in the y-direction. Solving for the components of initial velocity yields v_{x0} = 216.5 m/s, v_{y0} = 125 m/s. Setting up the y-direction displacement equation results in the following: $-5 = 125t_f - 4.9t_f^2$. Solving for t_f yields an impact time of around 25.5 seconds. To find the horizontal distance covered, simply set up the

Copyright © Mometrix Media. You have been licensed one copy of this document for personal use only. Any other reproduction or redistribution is strictly prohibited. All rights reserved.

displacement equation for the x-direction: $\Delta x = v_{x0}t_f + a_x t_f^2/2$. Since we ignore the effects of air resistance, acceleration in the x-direction is zero, yielding a flight distance of 5,530 m.

Uniform circular motion

We may say that a particle is in *uniform circular motion* when it is traveling in a circle, or circular arc, and at a constant speed. Crucially, we must note that such a particle is accelerating, even though the magnitude of its velocity does not change. This is because velocity is a vector, and consequently, any change in its direction is an acceleration. So, if we take two points on an arc of radius, r, separated by an angle, θ, and want to determine the time it will take a particle to move between these two points at a constant speed, $|v|$, we can use the equation: $\Delta t = r\theta/|v|$. The quantity $|v|/r$ is often written as ω, or angular velocity, having units of radians per second, so the time may also be computed as $\Delta t = \theta/\omega$. The speed, or absolute value of the velocity, of an object in uniform circular motion is also called the tangential speed, because the object is always moving in a direction tangent to the circle. Similarly, an increase in the magnitude of this velocity is called tangential acceleration.

A very important component of uniform motion is the centripetal acceleration. This is the acceleration that changes the direction of the velocity vector to follow the circular arc. It is directed toward the center of the circle or arc and is described by $a_c = |v|^2/r = r\omega^2$.

Relative motion and inertial reference frames

When we describe motion as being *relative*, we mean that it can only be measured in relation to something else. If a moving object is considered as it relates to some stationary object or arbitrary location, it will have a different measured velocity than it would if it were compared to some other object that is itself in motion. In other words, the measure of an object's velocity depends entirely on the reference frame from which the measurement is taken. When performing measurements of this kind, we may use any reference point we like. However, once we have decided on a reference point, we must be consistent in using it as the basis for all of our measurements, or else we will go astray. Additionally, if we want to be able to apply Newton's laws of motion or Galilean principles of relativity, we must select an inertial reference frame: that is, a reference frame that is not accelerating or rotating. A car traveling at a constant speed in a straight line is an inertial reference frame. A car moving in uniform circular motion is not.

An object's velocity with respect to a frame fixed to the earth can be computed by measuring its velocity from any inertial reference frame and combining that velocity by vector addition with the velocity of the inertial frame with respect to the earth. For instance, if a man is traveling in the x-direction at 20 m/s, and he throws a rock out the window at a relative velocity of 15 m/s in the y-direction, the rock's velocity with respect to the earth is found by adding the two vectors: $\mathbf{v_r} = 20\mathbf{i} + 15\mathbf{j}$ m/s.

Newton's Laws

Newton's first law

Before Newton formulated his laws of mechanics, it was generally assumed that some force had to act on an object continuously in order to make the object move at a constant velocity. Newton, however, determined that unless some other force acted on the object (most notably friction or air resistance), it would continue in the direction it was pushed at the same velocity forever. In this light, a body at rest and a body in motion are not all that different, and Newton's first law makes little distinction. It states that a body at rest will tend to remain at rest, while a body in motion will tend to remain in motion. This phenomenon is commonly referred to as inertia, the tendency of a

- 8 -

Copyright © Mometrix Media. You have been licensed one copy of this document for personal use only. Any other reproduction or redistribution is strictly prohibited. All rights reserved.

body to remain in its present state of motion. In order for the body's state of motion to change, it must be acted on by a non-zero net force. Net force is the vector sum of all forces acting on a body. If this vector sum is zero, then there is no unbalanced force, and the body will remain in its present state of motion. It is important to remember that this law only holds in inertial reference frames.

Newton's second law
Newton's second law states that an object's acceleration is directly proportional to the net force acting on the object, and inversely proportional to the object's mass. It is generally written in equation form $\mathbf{F} = m\mathbf{a}$, where $\mathbf{F}$ is the net force acting on a body, m is the mass of the body, and $\mathbf{a}$ is its acceleration. It is important to note from this equation that since the mass is always a positive quantity, the acceleration vector is always pointed in the same direction as the net force vector. Of course, in order to apply this equation correctly, one must clearly identify the body to which it is being applied. Once this is done, we may say that $\mathbf{F}$ is the vector sum of all forces acting on that body, or the net force. This measure includes only those forces that are external to the body; any internal forces, in which one part of the body exerts force on another, are discounted. Newton's second law somewhat encapsulates his first, because it includes the principle that if no net force is acting on a body, the body will not accelerate. As was the case with his first law, Newton's second law may only be applied in inertial reference frames.

Newton's third law
Newton's third law of motion is quite simple: for every force, there is an equal and opposite force. When a hammer strikes a nail, the nail hits the hammer just as hard. If we consider two objects, A and B, then we may express any contact between these two bodies with the equation $F_{AB} = -F_{BA}$. It is important to note in this kind of equation that the order of the subscripts denotes which body is exerting the force. Although the two forces are often referred to as the *action* and *reaction* forces, in physics there is really no such thing. There is no implication of cause and effect in the equation for Newton's third law. At first glance, this law might seem to forbid any movement at all. We must remember, however, that these equal, opposite forces are exerted on different bodies with different masses, so they will not cancel each other out.

Newton's law of gravitation
One of Newton's major insights into the behavior of physical objects was that every object in the universe exerts an attractive force on every other body. In quantitative terms, we may say that the gravitational force with which particles attract one another is given by $F = Gm_1m_2/r^2$, in which r is the distance between the particles and G is the gravitational constant, $G = 6.672 \times 10^{-11}$ N-m^2/kg^2. Although this equation is usually applied to particles, it may also be applied to objects, assuming that they are small relative to the distance between them. Newton expressed this relation by saying that a uniform spherical shell of matter attracts a particle outside the shell as if all the shell's matter were concentrated at its center. In the case of gravitation on earth, for instance, objects behave as if the earth were a single particle located at its center, and with the mass of the entire earth. Thus, regardless of an object's distance from the surface of the earth, it can be approximated as a particle due to the effective distance from the earth's center of mass. The difference in the gravitational pull on an object at sea level and that same object at the highest point on the earth's surface is about a quarter of a percent. Thus, the gravitational acceleration anywhere on the earth's surface is considered to be a constant, $g = 9.81$ m/s^2. For an object orbiting the earth, such as a satellite, its period of orbit can be found by equating the gravitational force to the centripetal force, giving the equation $Gm_em/r^2 = mr\omega^2 = mr(2pi/T)^2$. Solving for the period yields $T = sqrt(4pi^2r^3/Gm_e)$.

Copyright © Mometrix Media. You have been licensed one copy of this document for personal use only. Any other reproduction or redistribution is strictly prohibited. All rights reserved.

Static and kinetic frictional forces

In order to illustrate the concept of friction, let us imagine a book resting on a table. As it sits there, the force of its weight (W) is equal and opposite to the normal force (N). If, however, we were to exert a force (F) on the book, attempting to push it to one side, a frictional force (f) would arise, equal and opposite to our force. This kind of frictional force is known as *static frictional force*. As we increase our force on the book, however, we will eventually cause it to accelerate in the direction of our force. At this point, the frictional force opposing us will be known as *kinetic frictional force*. For the most part, kinetic frictional force is lower than static frictional force, and so the amount of force needed to maintain the movement of the book will be less than that needed to initiate movement. For wheels and spherical objects on a surface, static friction at the point of contact allows them to roll, but there is a frictional force that resists the rolling motion as well, due primarily to deformation effects in the rolling material. This is known as rolling friction, and tends to be much smaller than either static or kinetic friction.

Weight

Too often, weight is confused with mass. Strictly speaking, weight is the force pulling a body towards the center of a nearby astronomical body. Of course, in the case of most day-to-day operations for human beings, that astronomical body is the earth. The reason for weight is primarily a gravitational attraction between the masses of the two bodies. The SI unit for weight is the Newton. In general, we will be concerned with situations in which bodies with mass are located where the free-fall acceleration is g. In these situations, we may say that the magnitude of the weight vector is W = mg. As a vector, weight can be expressed as either -mg**j** or -W**j**, in which **j** is the direction on the axis pointing away from the earth.

Equilibrium

We may say that an object is in a state of equilibrium when it has a constant linear momentum P at its center of mass, and when angular momentum L is also constant about the center of mass. In other words, a wheel may be in equilibrium when it is spinning at a constant speed, and a hockey puck may be in equilibrium as it slides across ice. These are both examples of dynamic equilibrium. The phrase static equilibrium, however, is reserved for objects in which both linear and angular momentum are at zero. An object sitting on a table could be considered as being in static equilibrium.

Using equilibrium conditions

For a body in equilibrium, the net force vector and the net torque vector will both be equal to zero. For the most common cases, two-dimensional systems, these conditions can be fully expressed by one or two force summation equations and one torque summation equation. Torque summations may be taken about any point on the body, though strategic placement can make calculations simpler. To determine the torque exerted by a force, simply multiply the magnitude of the force by the perpendicular distance to the point of interest. It will be necessary to decide in advance which direction of torque (clockwise or counterclockwise) will be considered positive.

For example, if we have a bar of known mass, m, that is suspended by cables at each end and whose center of mass is two thirds of the way along its length, L, we can use the equilibrium conditions to determine the tension in each cable. Gravity exerts a force of $-mg$ on the bar's center of mass. Translational equilibrium conditions tell us that $T_1 + T_2 - mg = 0$. Setting the total torque about the

Copyright © Mometrix Media. You have been licensed one copy of this document for personal use only. Any other reproduction or redistribution is strictly prohibited. All rights reserved.

center of mass equal to zero, considering counterclockwise torque to be positive, yields the equation $T_2(L/3) - T_1(2L/3) = 0$. Solving these equations results in $T_1 = mg/3$ and $T_2 = 2mg/3$. This result makes sense since the center of mass is closer to the second cable.

Translational and rotational equilibrium

If a body is in translational equilibrium, then its linear momentum will be constant, and there will be a net force of zero. Likewise, a body in rotational equilibrium will have a constant angular momentum, and again there will be a net torque of zero. Both of these equations are vector equations, and as such are both equivalent to three scalar equations for the three dimensions of motion, though in most instances, only one or two dimensions will be considered at a time. We may say that the two requirements for a body to be in equilibrium are that the vector sum of all the external forces acting on the body must be zero, and the vector sum of all the external torques acting on the body must also be zero. Conversely, if we are told that a body is in equilibrium, we may assume that both of these conditions will hold, and that we can use them to find unknown forces or torques.

Friction

The first property of friction is that, if the body does not move when horizontal force F is applied, then the static frictional force is exactly equal and opposite to F. Static frictional force has a maximum value, however, which is expressed as $f_{s,max} = \mu_s N$, in which μ_s is the coefficient of static friction, and N is the magnitude of the normal force. If the magnitude of F should exceed the maximum value of static friction, the body will begin to move. Once the body has begun to slide, the frictional force will generally decrease. The value to which the frictional force will diminish is expressed as $f_k = \mu_k N$, in which μ_k is the coefficient of kinetic friction. For objects inclined to roll, such as balls or wheels, there is a rolling frictional force that resists the continued rolling of such an object. This force is expressed by $f_r = \mu_r N$, in which μ_r is the coefficient of rolling friction. All of these frictional coefficients are dimensionless. Since the value of the frictional force depends on the interaction of the body and the surface, it is usually described as friction between the two.

Basic equation for work

The equation for work (W) is fairly simple: $W = \mathbf{F} \cdot \mathbf{d}$, where $\mathbf{F}$ is the force exerted and $\mathbf{d}$ is the displacement of the object on which the force is exerted. For the simplest case, when the vectors of force and displacement have the same direction, the work done is equal to the product of the magnitudes of the force and displacement. If this is not the case, then the work may be calculated as $W = Fd \cos(\theta)$, where θ is the angle between the force and displacement vectors. If force and displacement have the same direction, then work is positive; if they are in opposite directions, however, work is negative; and if they are perpendicular, the work done by the force is zero.

For example, if a man pushes a block horizontally across a surface with a constant force of 10 N for a distance of 20 m, the work done by the man is 200 N-m or 200 J. If instead the block is sliding and the man tries to slow its progress by pushing against it, his work done is -200 J, since he is pushing in the direction opposite the motion. Also, if the man pushes vertically downward on the block while it slides, his work done is zero, since his force vector is perpendicular to the displacement vector of the block.

It is important to note in each of these cases that neither the mass of the block nor the elapsed time is considered when calculating the amount of work done by the man.

Copyright © Mometrix Media. You have been licensed one copy of this document for personal use only. Any other reproduction or redistribution is strictly prohibited. All rights reserved.

Polar coordinate system

Polar coordinates were designed to be useful in situations in which circular arcs are more common than straight lines and right angles. Instead of having x- and y-coordinates, an object's location is described by its distance from the origin, r, and the angle between its position vector and the positive x-axis, commonly denoted as θ.

The two coordinate systems are related by the following equations:

$x = r\cos(\theta)$, $y = r\sin(\theta)$

$r = \text{sqrt}(x^2 + y^2)$, $\theta = \tan^{-1}(y/x)$

The direction and nature of the conversion will dictate which set of equations to use.

The polar coordinate system simplifies many calculations of circular motion. Instead of a velocity in the x- or y-direction, velocity may be described by motion toward or away from the origin and an increase or decrease in the angle θ. For uniform circular motion, the change in r is zero, and the rate of change of angle θ is constant. The only acceleration on the body is the centripetal acceleration, given by $a_c = |v|^2/r = r\omega^2$, where ω is the rate of change in angle θ, known as the rotational velocity, keeping the body in its circular arc. This acceleration is caused by a centripetal force that pulls the object toward the center of the circle. By Newton's second law, this force has a magnitude given by $F = ma_c = m|v|^2/r = mr\omega^2$.

Power

Put simply, power is the rate at which work is done. Power, like work, is a scalar quantity. If we know the amount of work, W, that has been performed in a given amount of time, Δt, then we may find average power, $P_{av} = W/\Delta t$. If we are instead looking for the instantaneous power, there are two possibilities. If the force on an object is constant, and the object is moving at a constant velocity, then the instantaneous power is the same as the average power. If either the force or the velocity is varying, the instantaneous power should be computed by the equation $P = Fv$, where F and v are the instantaneous force and velocity. This equation may also be used to compute average power if the force and velocity are constant. Power is typically expressed in joules per second, or watts.

Kinetic energy

The kinetic energy of an object is that quality of its motion that can be related in a qualitative way to the amount of work performed on the object. Kinetic energy can be defined as $KE = mv^2/2$, in which m is the mass of an object and v is the magnitude of its velocity. Kinetic energy cannot be negative, since it depends on the square of velocity. Units for kinetic energy are the same as those for work: joules. Kinetic energy is a scalar quantity.

Changes in kinetic energy occur when a force does work on an object, such that the speed of the object is altered. This change in kinetic energy is equal to the amount of work that is done, and can be expressed as $W = KE_f - KE_i = \Delta KE$. This equation is commonly referred to as the work-kinetic energy theorem. If there are several different forces acting on the object, then W in this equation is

Copyright © Mometrix Media. You have been licensed one copy of this document for personal use only. Any other reproduction or redistribution is strictly prohibited. All rights reserved.

simply the total work done by all the forces, or by the net force. This equation can be very helpful in solving some problems that would otherwise rely solely on Newton's laws of motion.

Conservative and non-conservative forces

Forces that change the state of a system by changing kinetic energy into potential energy, or vice versa, are called conservative forces. This name arises because these forces conserve the total amount of kinetic and potential energy. Every other kind of force is considered non-conservative. One example of a conservative force is gravity. Consider the path of a ball thrown straight up into the air. Since the ball has the same amount of kinetic energy when it is thrown as it does when it returns to its original location (known as completing a closed path), gravity can be said to be a conservative force. More generally, a force can be said to be conservative if the work it does on an object through a closed path is zero. Frictional force would not meet this standard, of course, because it is only capable of performing negative work.

One-dimensional analysis of work done by a variable force

If the force on an object varies across the distance the object is moved, then a simple product will not yield the work. If we consider the work performed by a variable force in one dimension, then we are assuming that the directions of the force and the displacement are the same. The magnitude of the force will depend on the position of the particle. In order to calculate the amount of work performed by a variable force over a given distance, we should first divide the total displacement into a number of intervals, each with a width of Δx. We may then say that the amount of work performed during any one interval is $\Delta W = F_{av}\Delta x$, where F_{zv} is the average force over the interval Δx. We can then say that the total amount of work performed is the sum of all work performed during the various intervals. By reducing the interval to an infinitesimal length, we obtain the integral:

$$W = \int_{x_1}^{x_2} F_x dx$$

This integral requires that the force be a known function of x.

Hooke's law

The work performed by a spring is one of the classic examples of work performed by variable force. When a spring is neither compressed nor extended, we may say that it is in a relaxed state. Any time the spring is taken out of this state, whether by being stretched or compressed, it will exert what is called a restoring force, as it attempts to return to its relaxed state. In most cases, we can say that the force, F, exerted by the spring is proportional to the displacement of the free end from its position during the relaxed state. This is known as Hooke's law, and is expressed $F = -kx$, where k is the spring constant or stiffness. The x-coordinate in this equation corresponds to an axis where $x = 0$ is the coordinate of the relaxed position. The negative sign in this equation indicates that the force is always opposite to the displacement.

Potential energy

Potential energy is the amount of energy that can be ascribed to a body or bodies based on configuration. There are a couple of different kinds of potential energy. Gravitational potential energy is the energy associated with the separation of bodies that are attracted to one another gravitationally. Any time you lift an object, you are increasing its gravitational potential energy.

Copyright © Mometrix Media. You have been licensed one copy of this document for personal use only. Any other reproduction or redistribution is strictly prohibited. All rights reserved.

Gravitational potential energy can be found by the equation PE = mgh, where m is the mass of an object, g is the gravitational acceleration, and h is its height above a reference point, most often the ground.

Another kind of potential energy is elastic potential energy; elastic potential energy is associated with the compression or expansion of an elastic, or spring-like, object. Physicists will often refer to potential energy as being stored within a body, the implication being that it could emerge in the future.

Work performed by a spring

If we are to move a block attached to a spring from point x_i to point x_f, we can be said to be doing work on the block, as the spring is also doing work on the block. To determine the work done by the spring on the block, we can substitute F from Hooke's law into our equation for work performed by a variable force, and arrive at this measure: $W = k(x_i^2 - x_f^2)/2$. This work will be positive if $x_i^2 > x_f^2$, and negative if the opposite is true. If $x_i = 0$ and we decide to call the final position x, then we may change our equation: $W = -kx^2/2$. It is important to keep in mind that this is the work done by the spring. The work done by the force that moves the block to its final position will be a positive quantity.

Like all simple harmonic oscillators, springs operate by storing and releasing potential energy. The amount of energy being stored or released by a spring is equal to the magnitude of the work done by the spring during that same operation. The total potential energy stored in a spring can be calculated as $PE = kx^2/2$. Neglecting the effects of friction and drag, an object oscillating on a spring will continue to do so indefinitely, since total mechanical energy (kinetic and potential) is conserved. In such a situation, the period of oscillation can be calculated as $T = 2pi*sqrt(m/k)$.

Simple harmonic motion

Simple harmonic motion in a single dimension, x, can be described by the equation $x = Acos(\omega t + \varphi)$, where A is the amplitude of oscillation, ω is the angular frequency of oscillation, and φ is the phase. The particular trigonometric operator used in the equation is not of great importance as sine may be substituted for cosine given a proper modification of the phase. Graphically, the motion of a harmonic oscillator starting from rest at maximum displacement is shown by the graph below. This graph assumes no energy lost to friction or drag.

Linear momentum and impulse

In physics, linear momentum can be found by multiplying the mass and velocity of a particle: $P = mv$. Momentum has units of kg-m/s. Like velocity, momentum is a vector quantity and will always have the same direction as the velocity. Newton's second law describes momentum, stating that the rate of change of momentum is proportional to the force exerted, and is in the direction of the force. Impulse is the application of force over a period of time. If a constant net force of 10 N is exerted on an object for 5 seconds, it gives the object an impulse of 50 N-s. An impulse of 50 N-s corresponds to a change in momentum of 50 kg-m/s in the direction of the force. In equation form, $Ft = \Delta mv$, where F is a constant net force. If the force is varying, it will be necessary to integrate the force over time.

For example, suppose a 2-kg block is initially at rest on a frictionless surface and a constant net force of 8 N is exerted on the block for 5 seconds. In order to determine how fast the block is

Copyright © Mometrix Media. You have been licensed one copy of this document for personal use only. Any other reproduction or redistribution is strictly prohibited. All rights reserved.

moving, we need to calculate the impulse that was given to it, $Ft = 40$ N-s. This means that the change in momentum of the block was 40 kg-m/s. Since the block has a mass of 2 kg, this translates to an increase in velocity of 20 m/s. Thus, the block will be traveling at 20 m/s after 5 seconds.

Simple pendulum

A pendulum is a harmonic oscillator that depends on the force of gravity for its motion. If we consider a simple pendulum composed of a mass hanging from an inelastic, massless string, then we may describe its restoring force as $F = -mg \sin(\theta)$, in which θ is the angle by which the mass is removed from its resting position. If the angle is very small, less than 15° or pi/12, then $\theta \approx \sin(\theta)$, and the motion of the pendulum is like that of a simple harmonic oscillator. If this is the case, then the period of our simple pendulum can be found as $T = 2pi*sqrt(L/g)$, where L is the length of the string. Again, this only holds if the angular amplitude θ_{max} is very small.

Like springs, pendulums operate by converting energy between kinetic and potential. Unlike springs, the potential energy stored in pendulums is gravitational potential energy. As the mass is displaced from its resting state, its height above ground increases. The potential energy stored in a simple pendulum can be calculated as $PE = mgL(1 - \cos(\theta))$.

Examples of one-dimensional collisions

All examples assume a frictionless surface.

If a 0.01-kg bullet traveling at 400 m/s strikes a stationary 10-kg block of wood, and buries itself in the wood, find the final velocity of the block and the bullet.

The bullet initially has 4 kg-m/s of momentum. The block of wood, beginning at rest, has no momentum. Thus, the final momentum is 4 kg-m/s. Given the new combined mass of 10.01 kg, the final velocity is approximately 0.4 m/s.

Two blocks, having masses of 10 kg and 40 kg, are traveling toward one another with velocities of - 20 m/s and 10 m/s, respectively. If the collision was perfectly elastic, find the final velocities of each body. If it was perfectly inelastic, find the final velocity of the resulting single body.

For elastic collisions, two conditions hold: $KE_i = KE_f$ and $P_i = P_f$. Calculating initial conditions yields $KE_i = 4000$ J and $P_i = 200$ kg-m/s total for both blocks. Equating these to the final values of each yields $5v_{1f}^2 + 20v_{2f}^2 = 4000$ and $10v_{1f} + 40v_{2f} = 200$. Solving both equations simultaneously gives v_{1f} = 28 m/s and v_{2f} = -2 m/s.

The inelastic case is much simpler. Since the two blocks merge to form one, the final momentum, 200 kg-m/s, is divided by the combined mass to give the final velocity of 4 m/s.

Linear momentum and collisions

If we assume a closed and isolated system (that is, one in which no particles leave or enter, and on which the sum of external forces is zero), then we can assume that the momentum of the system will neither increase nor decrease. That is, if we write the equation for the linear momentum of the system such that the net external force $F_{ext} = 0$, then we will find that linear momentum, P, is a constant. The equation for linear momentum is a vector equation, and as such it can be divided into component equations for each dimension.

Copyright © Mometrix Media. You have been licensed one copy of this document for personal use only. Any other reproduction or redistribution is strictly prohibited. All rights reserved.

Some of the most popular examples to demonstrate conservation of linear momentum involve two objects colliding on a frictionless surface. A perfectly elastic collision is one in which both total momentum and kinetic energy are conserved. A perfectly inelastic collision is one in which only momentum is conserved, as the two bodies combine to form a single body. Most actual collisions fall somewhere between these two extremes. Unless a collision is specified as being elastic, it should be assumed that only momentum is conserved.

Angular motion and the axis of rotation

When a body is moving in a straight line, it is said to be moving in translation. When, on the other hand, it is moving around some fixed axis, it is said to be in rotation. For a rotating object, the fixed axis is called the axis of rotation. Every point on the body will move in a circle that has this axis as its center, and every point will move through the same angle over the same interval of time. Angles may be measured in one of three units: degrees, radians, or revolutions. A full rotation is equal to 360 degrees, 2pi radians, or 1 revolution. On a circle, one radian is the angle that measures an arc length equal to the radius of the circle. Since a circle's circumference is 2pi times the radius, one full rotation is equal to 2pi radians.

Angular motion has many correlations to linear motion. For an angle of rotation, θ, the linear distance traveled is $x = r\theta$. For angular velocity, ω, the linear velocity is $v = r\omega$. For angular acceleration, α, the linear acceleration is $a = r\alpha$. When discussing angular motion in this way, the angular unit is always radians.

Two-dimensional collisions

All examples assume a frictionless surface.

Two blocks of mass, 5 kg and 10 kg, having velocities $v_1 = 9i$ m/s and $v_2 = 3j$ m/s, respectively, are on a collision course. If the collision is perfectly inelastic, find the velocity of the combined block after collision.

Since each block initially has velocity in only one dimension, it is a simple calculation to find intial momentum values: $P_x = 45$ kg-m/s and $P_y = 30$ kg-m/s. With the new combined mass of 15 kg, the final velocity vector will be $v_f = 3i + 2j$ m/s.

Two hockey pucks, each with a mass of 0.15 kg, having velocity vectors $v_1 = 20i + 30j$ m/s and $v_2 = -50i - 10j$ m/s, are headed toward a collision. If the final velocity of one puck is $v_{2f} = -10i + 15j$ m/s, find the final velocity vector of the other puck.

We must ensure that momentum is conserved in both dimensions. The initial momentum in the x- and y-directions is calculated to be $P_{xi} = -4.5$ kg-m/s and $P_{yi} = 3$ kg-m/s. Since we know the final velocity of one of the pucks, we can find the other's final velocity to be $v_{1f} = -20i + 5j$ m/s.

Applying conservation of energy and momentum

A metal hoop of mass m and radius r is released from rest at the top of a hill of height h. Assuming that it rolls without sliding and does not lose energy to friction or drag, what will be the hoop's angular and linear velocities upon reaching the bottom of the hill?

Copyright © Mometrix Media. You have been licensed one copy of this document for personal use only. Any other reproduction or redistribution is strictly prohibited. All rights reserved.

The hoop's initial energy is all potential energy, $PE = mgh$. As the hoop rolls down, all of its energy is converted to translational and rotational kinetic energy. Thus, $mgh = mv^2/2 + I\omega^2/2$. Since the moment for a hoop is $I = mr^2$, and $\omega = v/r$, the equation may be rewritten as $mgh = mv^2/2 + mr^2(v^2/r^2)/2$, which further simplifies to $mgh = mv^2$. Thus, the resulting velocity of the hoop is $v_f = \mathrm{sqrt}(gh)$, with an angular velocity of $\omega_f = v_f/r$. Note that if you were to forget about the energy converted to rotational motion, you would calculate a final velocity of $v_f = \mathrm{sqrt}(2gh)$, which is the impact velocity of an object dropped from height h.

Consider a planet orbiting the sun through an elliptical orbit with small radius r_S and large radius r_L. Find the angular velocity of the planet when it is at distance r_S from the sun if its velocity at r_L is ω_L.

Since the size of a planet is almost insignificant compared to the interplanetary distances, the planet may be treated as a single particle of mass m, giving it a moment about the sun of $I = mr^2$. Since the gravitational force is incapable of exerting a net torque on an object, we can assume that the planet's angular momentum about the sun is a constant. Thus, $mr_L^2\omega_L = mr_S^2\omega_S$. Solving this equation for ω_S yields $\omega_S = \omega_L(r_L^2/r_S^2)$.

Rotational motion

Newton's second law, commonly stated as $F = ma$, is applied to rotational motion by the equation $\tau = I\alpha$. That is, the torque is equal to the moment of inertia times the angular acceleration. Torque is calculated as the magnitude of an applied force times its perpendicular distance from the body's center of mass. A body's moment of inertia depends on both its mass and its configuration. Each particle in a body contributes a moment of $I = mr^2$, where m is the particle's mass and r is its distance from the center of mass. Thus, for a thin ring or a thin hollow sphere, the moment for the body is $I = mr^2$. Some other commonly encountered shapes are spheres ($I = (2/5)mr^2$) and disks ($I = (1/2)mr^2$). A closely related property of these shapes is the radius of gyration, k. This quantity is the average distance of mass from the center. It can be found by the equation $k = \mathrm{sqrt}(I/m)$. Similarly, the moment of inertia may be found as $I = mk^2$.

Another important corollary with linear motion is momentum. An object's angular momentum may be calculated as $L = I\omega$. All the same conservation rules for linear momentum apply to angular momentum as well. Additionally, there is a kinetic energy associated with rotational motion. It is calculated as $KE_r = I\omega^2/2$. When calculating kinetic energy for an object that is in both linear and angular motion, the total kinetic energy is the sum of the translational and rotational kinetic energy, $KE = mv^2/2 + I\omega^2/2$.

Mass-energy relationship

Because mass consists of atoms, which are themselves formed of subatomic particles, there is an energy inherent in the composition of all mass. If all the atoms in a given mass were formed from their most basic particles, it would require a significant input of energy. This rest energy is the energy that Einstein refers to in his famous mass-energy relation $E = mc^2$, where c is the speed of light in a vacuum. In theory, if all the subatomic particles in a given mass were to spontaneously split apart, it would give off energy $E = mc^2$. For example, if this were to happen to a single gram of mass, the resulting outburst of energy would be $E = 9 \times 10^{13}$ J, enough energy to heat more than 200,000 cubic meters of water from the freezing point to the boiling point.

Copyright © Mometrix Media. You have been licensed one copy of this document for personal use only. Any other reproduction or redistribution is strictly prohibited. All rights reserved.

In some nuclear reactions, small amounts of mass are converted to energy. The amount of energy released can be calculated through the same relation, $E = mc^2$. Most such reactions involve mass losses on the order of 10^{-30} kg.

Kepler's Laws

Kepler's First Law

Kepler's first law describing the movement of planets states that all planets move in elliptical orbits, with the sun at one focus. If we are to consider the motion of one planet around the sun, we will assume that its mass is much smaller than that of the sun, such that the center of mass of the system is almost in the middle of the sun. The orbit of the planet will then be defined by the semimajor axis, a (that is, half the length of the ellipse), the semiminor axis, b (half the width of the ellipse), and the eccentricity, e (the degree to which the orbit is not circular, $e = sqrt(1-b^2/a^2)$). The orbits of the planets are only slightly elliptical, though they are often exaggerated on diagrams. In a planetary orbit, the distance from the center of the ellipse to either focus is d = ae. The maximum and minimum distances of a planet from the sun are given by $r_{max} = b^2/(a - d)$ and $r_{min} = b^2/(a + d)$.

Kepler's Second Law

Kepler's second law for planets and satellites states that any line connecting a planet to the sun will sweep out equal areas in equal times, regardless of where the planet is in its orbit. In other words, the planet will move most slowly when it is far away from the sun, and fastest when it is closest. This law says basically the same thing as the law of conservation of angular momentum.

Kepler's Third Law

Kepler's third law for planets states that the square of the period of any planet is proportional to the cube of the semimajor axis of its orbit. This relation can be expressed $T^2 = (4pi^2/Gm)r^3$. The quantity in parentheses in this equation is a constant, its only variable being the mass of the central body. This equation holds up for elliptical orbits as well.

Fluids

Basics of fluids

It sounds obvious, perhaps, but fluids can best be defined as substances that flow. A fluid will conform, slowly or quickly, to any container in which it is placed. This is because a fluid is unable to maintain a force tangential to its surface. In other words, fluids cannot withstand shearing stress. They can, on the other hand, exert a force perpendicular to their surface. Both liquids and gases are considered to be fluids. Fluids, essentially, are those substances in which the atoms are not arranged in any permanent, rigid way. In ice, for instance, molecules are all lined up in a crystalline lattice, while in water and steam the only intermolecular arrangements are haphazard connections between neighboring molecules.

Fluid density and pressure

The density of a fluid is generally expressed with the symbol ρ. The density may be found with the simple equation $\rho = m/V$, mass per unit volume. Density is a scalar property, meaning that it has no direction component. It is typically measured in SI units of kilograms per cubic meter. While the density of a gas will tend to fluctuate considerably depending on the level of pressure, the density of a liquid is comparatively stable. The density of water is most often taken to be 1000 kg/m^3.

The pressure of a fluid is calculated as P = F/A, force per unit area. To find the pressure at a given depth in a fluid, or the hydrostatic pressure, the pressure can be calculated as $P = \rho gh$, where h is

- 18 -

Copyright © Mometrix Media. You have been licensed one copy of this document for personal use only. Any other reproduction or redistribution is strictly prohibited. All rights reserved.

the fluid depth. Pressure, like fluid density, is a scalar, and does not have a direction. The equation for pressure is concerned only with the magnitude of that force, not with the direction in which it is pointing. The SI unit of pressure is the Newton per square meter, or pascal.

Ideal fluids in motion

Since the motion of actual fluids is extremely complex, physicists usually refer to ideal fluids when they make their calculations. Using ideal fluids in equations is a bit like discounting friction in other calculations; it tends to make the process more mathematically manageable. So, when we deal with ideal fluids, we are making four assumptions. First, we are assuming that the flow is steady; in other words, the velocity of every part of the fluid is the same. Second, we assume that fluids are incompressible, and therefore have a consistent density. Third, we assume that fluids are nonviscous, meaning that they flow easily and without resistance. Finally, we assume that the flow of ideal fluids is irrotational: that is, particles in the fluid will not rotate around a center of mass.

Streamlines, tube of flow, volume flow rate, and the equation of continuity

A streamline is the path traced out by a very small unit of fluid, which we will refer to as a particle. Although the velocity of a particle may change in both magnitude and direction, streamlines will never cross one another. In many instances of flow, several streamlines will group together to form what is called a tube of flow. If we were to make two cross-sections of a tube of flow, with areas A_1 and A_2, we would find that since fluid is incompressible, the same amount of fluid passes through the two cross-sections over the same interval of time. This is expressed by the equation $Q = Av$, in which Q is known as the volumetric flow rate and is constant for a given tube of flow. This equation is known as the equation of continuity; it suggests that flow will be faster in areas of the tube that are narrower. One very important equation derived from this principle is $A_1v_1 = A_2v_2$. Given that a pipe narrows its cross-section from A_1 to A_2, and the fluid velocity in A_1 is v_1, the velocity in A_2 must be $v_2 = A_1v_1/A_2$. Also important to note is that the mass flow rate is directly related to the volumetric flow rate by the equation $m_{flow} = \rho vA = \rho Q$.

Bernoulli's equation

Let us imagine an ideal fluid in a tube of flow. By applying the law of conservation of energy with ideal fluid assumptions, we can arrive at what is known as Bernoulli's equation: $P + \rho gh + \rho v^2/2 = C$, where C is a constant for a given tube of flow. Basically, this equation states that in the absence of an external input of energy or a significant elevation change, any increase in velocity will require a decrease in fluid pressure. And under similar circumstances, an increase in pressure will necessarily cause a decrease in velocity. It is essentially just a reformulation of the law of conservation of mechanical energy for fluid mechanics. Bernoulli's principle is used to explain a number of physical phenomena, including the lift force on the wings of an aircraft.

Archimedes' principle

If an object is submerged in water, it will have a buoyant force exerted on it in the upward direction. This force is caused by the water pressure acting on the bottom surface of the object. The deeper the object is submerged, the greater the pressure at the bottom surface. Often, of course, this buoyant force is much too small to keep an object from sinking to the bottom. This idea of buoyancy is summarized in Archimedes' principle: a body wholly or partially submerged in a fluid will be buoyed up by a force equal to the weight of the fluid displaced by the body. Thus, an object's ability to remain afloat in a fluid depends on its density relative to that of the fluid. If the fluid has a higher density than the object, it will float. Otherwise, it will sink. This principle can also be used to find the weight of a floating object by calculating the volume of fluid that it has displaced. For instance if a cube with a volume of 1 m³ is floating in water to a depth of 0.25 m, the cube is

Copyright © Mometrix Media. You have been licensed one copy of this document for personal use only. Any other reproduction or redistribution is strictly prohibited. All rights reserved.

displacing 0.25 m³ of water. This is the equivalent of 250 kg of water, creating a buoyancy force of 2450 N. Thus, the block weighs 2450 N, has a mass of 250 kg, and has a density of 250 kg/m³.

Pascal's principle

Pascal's principle states that a change in the pressure applied to an enclosed fluid is transmitted undiminished to every portion of the fluid, as well as to the walls of the containing vessel. Imagine, for instance, a container filled with liquid, on top of which rests a piston loaded down with a lead weight. The atmosphere, lead weight, and piston will combine to exert pressure P_{ext} on the liquid, so the total pressure will be $P = P_{ext} + \rho gh$, for every point at height h within the fluid. Imagine again, an enclosed fluid in a container with two pistons on top, one with area $A_1 = 2$ m² and the other with area $A_2 = 4$ m². Since the pressure will be the same at both pistons, the upward force on the larger piston will be twice that of the smaller, since it has a larger area and the force is equal to the pressure times the area over which it is applied.

Copyright © Mometrix Media. You have been licensed one copy of this document for personal use only. Any other reproduction or redistribution is strictly prohibited. All rights reserved.

Thermodynamics, Atomic and Modern Physics

Temperature scales

Each of the temperature scales, Celsius and Fahrenheit, has a corresponding absolute temperature scale, Kelvin and Rankine, respectively. A temperature of zero Kelvin or zero Rankine is known as absolute zero, at which point there is theoretically no atomic motion or thermal energy. Kelvins and degrees Celsius are related by the equation, $T \,°C = (T + 273.15) \,K$. Similarly, Rankines and degrees Fahrenheit are related as $T \,°F = (T + 459.67) \,R$. From these relations, we can see that within both individual pairs of temperature scales, the magnitude of the unit is the same; that is, an increase of 1 °C is the same an increase of 1 K, while an increase of 1 °F equals an increase of 1 R. Converting from Fahrenheit to Celsius is slightly more complicated: $T \,°F = (5/9)(T - 32) \,°C$, or in reverse, $T \,°C = ((9/5)T + 32) \,°F$. From these equations, we can see that a degree Celsius is greater than a degree Fahrenheit.

Heat and temperature

Heat, or thermal energy, is a measure of the kinetic energy of the atoms within a substance. Heat, being a form of energy, has SI units of joules, but is also commonly measured in calories. The amount of heat a substance contains is generally quantified as a temperature. Temperature has SI units of degrees Celsius, though degrees Fahrenheit are also widely used.

It is often useful to know how much heat is required to cause a certain amount of material to reach a desired temperature. Each material has a property called specific heat, which allows this calculation. To bring about a temperature increase ΔT to a mass m made of a material with specific heat C, the required heat input is found by the equation $Q = mC\Delta T$. This equation can also be used to calculate the amount of heat absorbed during a given temperature increase. The amount of heat required to raise the temperature of a gram of water by one degree Celsius, or one Kelvin, is one calorie, or 4.184 J. Thus, the specific heat of water is 1 cal/g-K.

Latent heat and specific heat

Suppose we wish to convert ice initially at -5 °C to water at 5 °C. We must provide heat to accomplish this. The amount of heat required to raise the temperature of a given quantity of a material is a property known as specific heat. This is most often given on a mass basis, with units of J/g-K, but may also be given as a molar property as J/mol-K. If the given quantity of material and the given specific heat are not unit compatible, it will be necessary to multiply or divide by the molar weight of the material to achieve compatibility. Returning to the problem at hand, in order for ice initially at -5 °C to reach 5 °C, it must undergo a phase change, from a solid to a liquid. When the ice is heated, it does not simply become water when it reaches 0 °C. In order for the ice to become water, additional heat must be added to break the bonds of the solid. This heat is called the latent heat of fusion and, like the specific heat, may be given on a mass or a molar basis, with common units of kJ/g or kJ/mol, respectively. This heat input for the phase change occurs while the material remains at a constant temperature. Once the phase change has been completed, the water temperature will begin to rise again with heat input, though the specific heat of liquid water will be different from that of ice. If the water need be heated above 100 °C, it will have to undergo a second phase change, overcoming the latent heat of vaporization, and its temperature will subsequently be governed by a third specific heat, that of the gas phase.

Copyright © Mometrix Media. You have been licensed one copy of this document for personal use only. Any other reproduction or redistribution is strictly prohibited. All rights reserved.

Thermal expansion

When heated, most materials will undergo some amount of expansion. Though this is generally quite small, it is important to know how much of an impact this thermal expansion might have on the size of the object in question. Each material has a linear coefficient of thermal expansion α, generally having units of $1/^\circ C$ or $1/^\circ F$, that relates the additional length to the original length. The percentage change in length is found by the equation $\Delta L/L_0 = \alpha\Delta T$, or to find the absolute change, $\Delta L = L_0\alpha\Delta T$. Just as heating the material causes it to expand, cooling it will cause it to contract. Assuming that the material is able to expand in all directions, there will similarly be a change in areas and volumes. The change in an area A_0 will be $\Delta A = 2\alpha A_0\Delta T + \alpha^2\Delta T^2$. Because α is generally much less than 1, $\alpha^2\Delta T^2$ will most often be negligible. Thus the change in area becomes $\Delta A = 2\alpha A_0\Delta T$. From this we can see that the area coefficient of thermal expansion is $\gamma = 2\alpha$, and $\Delta A = \gamma A_0\Delta T$. By making similar assumptions with the equation for change in volume, we find that the volume coefficient of thermal expansion is $\beta = 3\alpha$ and that $\Delta V = \beta V_0\Delta T$.

Convection

Heat always flows from a region of higher temperature to a region of lower temperature. If two regions are at the same temperature, there is a thermal equilibrium between them and there will be no net heat transfer between them. Convection is a mode of heat transfer in which a surface in contact with a fluid experiences a heat flow. The heat rate for convection is given as $q = hA\Delta T$, where h is the convection coefficient. The convection coefficient is dependent on a number of factors, including the configuration of the surface and the nature and velocity of the fluid. For complicated configurations, it often has to be determined experimentally.

Convection may be classified as either free or forced. In free convection, when a surface transfers heat to the surrounding air, the heated air becomes less dense and rises, allowing cooler air to descend and come into contact with the surface. Free convection may also be called natural convection. Forced convection in this example would involve forcibly cycling the air: for instance, with a fan. While this does generally require an additional input of work, the convection coefficient is always greater for forced convection.

Conduction

Heat always flows from a region of higher temperature to a region of lower temperature. If two regions are at the same temperature, there is a thermal equilibrium between them and there will be no net heat transfer between them. Conduction is a form of heat transfer that requires contact. Since heat is a measure of kinetic energy, most commonly vibration, at the atomic level, it may be transferred from one location to another or one object to another by contact. The rate at which heat is transferred is proportional to the material's thermal conductivity k, cross-sectional area A, and temperature gradient dT/dx, $q = kA(dT/dx)$. If two ends of a rod are each held at a constant temperature, the heat transfer through the rod will be given as $q = kA(T_H - T_L)/d$, where d is the length of the rod. The heat will flow from the hot end to the cold end. The thermal conductivity is generally given in units of W/m-K. Metals are some of the best conductors, many having a thermal conductivity around 400 W/m-K. The thermal conductivity of wood is very small, generally less than 0.5 W/m-k. Diamond is extremely thermally conductive and may have a conductivity of over 2,000 W/m-k. Although fluids also have thermal conductivity, they will tend to transfer heat primarily through convection.

Copyright © Mometrix Media. You have been licensed one copy of this document for personal use only. Any other reproduction or redistribution is strictly prohibited. All rights reserved.

Kinetic molecular theory

The kinetic molecular theory of gases states that the pressure exerted by a gas is due to numerous collisions of molecules with one another and with container walls. This assertion led to the development of what is now known as the ideal gas law: $PV = nRT$, where P is pressure, V is volume, T is temperature, n is the number of moles of gas present, and R is the universal gas constant. Different aspects of this law have different names, but there are many simple relations that may be derived from it. For instance, if an ideal gas is contained such that no molecules can escape, then it may be said that $P_1V_1/T_1 = P_2V_2/T_2$, where the subscripts indicate distinct sets of conditions. Generally, one of the three variables will be held constant while the other two change. If an ideal gas in a container with a constant volume is heated, the effect this has on the pressure can be determined both analytically and numerically. Additional energy imparted to the gas particles will cause them to move faster and, by the kinetic molecular theory, faster particles mean more collisions and a higher resulting pressure. Numerically, $P_1/T_1 = P_2/T_2$. This means that if T_2 is higher than T_1, then P_2 must be equivalently higher than P_1 to maintain the same ratio. Other derivations from the ideal gas law include calculating molarity or moles per unit volume ($n/V = P/RT$), gas density if the molecular weight M is known ($\rho = PM/RT$), or conversely, molecular weight if the density is known ($M = \rho RT/P$).

Radiation

Heat always flows from a region of higher temperature to a region of lower temperature. If two regions are at the same temperature, there is a thermal equilibrium between them and there will be no net heat transfer between them. Radiation heat transfer occurs via electromagnetic radiation between two bodies. Unlike conduction and convection, radiation requires no medium in which to take place. Indeed, the heat we receive from the sun is entirely radiation since it must pass through a vacuum to reach us. Every body at a temperature above absolute zero emits heat radiation at a rate given by the equation $q = e\sigma AT^4$, where e is the surface emissivity and σ is the Stefan-Boltzmann constant. The net radiation heat-transfer rate for a body is given by $q = e\sigma A(T^4 - T_0^4)$, where T_0 is the temperature of the surroundings. Emissivity, which has a value between 0 and 1, is a measure of how well a surface absorbs and emits radiation. Dark-colored surfaces tend to have high emissivity, while shiny or reflective surfaces have low emissivity. In the radiation heat-rate equation, it is important to remember to use absolute temperature units, since the temperature value is being raised to a power.

Laws of Thermodynamics

First law
The first law of thermodynamics states that energy cannot be created or destroyed, but only converted from one form to another. It is generally applied as $Q = \Delta U + W$, where Q is the net heat energy added to a system, ΔU is the change in internal energy of the system, and W is the work done by the system. For any input of heat energy to a system, that energy must be either converted to internal energy through a temperature increase or expended in doing work. For a system that gives off heat, either the temperature of the system must decrease or work must be done on the system by its surroundings. By convention, work done by the system is positive while work done on the system is negative.

For instance, suppose a gas is compressed by a piston while the gas temperature remains constant. If we consider the gas to be the system, the work is negative, since the work is being performed on the gas. Since the temperature remains constant, $\Delta U = 0$. Thus Q must be a negative quantity,

Copyright © Mometrix Media. You have been licensed one copy of this document for personal use only. Any other reproduction or redistribution is strictly prohibited. All rights reserved.

indicating that heat is lost by the gas. Conversely, if the gas does positive work on the piston while remaining at a constant temperature, the gas must be receiving heat input from the surroundings.

Second law

The second law of thermodynamics is primarily a statement of the natural tendency of all things toward disorder rather than order. It deals with a quantity called entropy, which is an inverse measure of the remaining useful energy in a system. If we take a system of a pot of hot water and an ice cube, the system entropy initially has a value of s_1. After the ice cube melts in the water and the system reaches an equilibrium temperature, the system has larger entropy value s_2, which is the maximum entropy for the system. The system cannot return to its initial state without work input to refreeze the ice cube and reheat the water. If this is done and the system returns to a state with entropy s_1, then the entropy of the surroundings must at the same time increase by more than $s_2 - s_1$, since the net entropy from any process is always greater than zero. Reversible processes are those that may be accomplished in reverse without requiring additional work input. These processes do not exist in the real world, but can be useful for approximating some situations. All real processes are irreversible, meaning they require additional work input to accomplish in reverse. Another important concept is that of spontaneity, the ability of a process to occur without instigation. An ice cube located in an environment at a temperature above the freezing point will spontaneously melt. Although some processes can decrease system entropy at a cost to the entropy of the surroundings, all spontaneous processes involve an increase in system entropy.

Third and zeroth laws

The third law of thermodynamics regards the behavior of systems as they approach absolute zero temperature. Actually reaching a state of absolute zero is impossible. According to this law, all activity disappears as molecules slow to a standstill near absolute zero, and the system achieves a perfect crystal structure while the system entropy approaches its minimum value. For most systems, this would in fact be a value of zero entropy. Note that this does not violate the second law since causing a system to approach absolute zero would require an immense increase in the entropy of the surroundings, resulting in a positive net entropy. This law is used to determine the value of a material's standard entropy, which is its entropy value at the standard temperature of 25 °C.

The zeroth law of thermodynamics deals with thermal equilibrium between two systems. It states that if two systems are both in thermal equilibrium with a third system, then they are in thermal equilibrium with each other. This may seem intuitive, but it is an important basis for the other thermodynamic laws.

Thermodynamic processes of gases

In discussing thermodynamic processes applied to gases, it is important to understand what is meant by some of the different types of processes that can take place. Most real processes do not strictly hold to one of these types, but most can be reasonably approximated by one of them. A process in which the pressure remains constant is known as an isobaric process. In this type of process, the volume-to-absolute-temperature ratio remains constant. In an isothermal process, the temperature remains constant, as does the product of the pressure and volume. For isothermal processes, the internal energy of the gas is constant and, by the first law of thermodynamics, the heat added is equal to the work done by the gas. An adiabatic process is one in which no heat is transferred between the gas or its surroundings. This does not mean that the temperature of the gas remains the same, but only that any temperature changes are due to changes in pressure or

- 24 -

Copyright © Mometrix Media. You have been licensed one copy of this document for personal use only. Any other reproduction or redistribution is strictly prohibited. All rights reserved.

volume or, by the first law, the change in internal energy of the gas is equal to the amount of work done on the gas by its surroundings.

Heat engines and the Carnot cycle

A heat engine is a mechanical device that takes in heat energy Q_H from a high-temperature region, uses that energy to produce work W, and then expels heat Q_C to a lower-temperature region. When the machine is operating at steady state, such that it does not change temperature, the first law of thermodynamics tells us that the net heat input is equal to the work achieved, $Q_H - Q_C = W$. We can define the efficiency of a heat engine as the work received divided by the work put in, or $\eta = W/Q_H$. The rejected heat Q_C is not considered work received because it is not usable for work. The efficiency may also be calculated as $\eta = 1 - Q_C/Q_H$. From this, we can see that 100% efficiency can only be achieved if $Q_C = 0$. However, constructing a heat engine that expels no heat is impossible. A Carnot engine is a heat engine that operates on the Carnot cycle, an ideal reversible gas cycle that consists of the following processes: high-temperature isothermal expansion, adiabatic expansion, low-temperature isothermal compression, and adiabatic compression. The efficiency of this ideal engine is given as $\eta = 1 - T_C/T_H$, where T_C and T_H are the low and high temperatures of the gas during the cycle. Carnot's theorem states that no he
at engine operating between T_C and T_H can have a higher efficiency than that of the Carnot engine.

Conversion of energy

There are many different types of energy that exist. These include mechanical, sound, magnetic, electrical, light, heat, and chemical. From the first law of thermodynamics, we know that no energy can be created or destroyed, but it may be converted from one form to another. This does not mean that all forms of energy are useful. Indeed, the second law states that net useful energy decreases in every process that takes place. Most often this occurs when other forms of energy are converted to heat through means such as friction. In these cases, the heat is quickly absorbed into the surroundings and becomes unusable. There are many examples of energy conversion, such as in an automobile. The chemical energy in the gasoline is converted to mechanical energy in the engine. Subsequently, this mechanical energy is converted to kinetic energy as the car moves. Additionally, the mechanical energy is converted to electrical energy to power the radio, headlights, air conditioner, and other devices. In the radio, electrical energy is converted to sound energy. In the headlights, it is converted to heat and light energy. In the air conditioner, it does work to remove heat energy from the car's interior. It is important to remember that, in all of these processes, a portion of the energy is lost from its intended purpose.

Thomson "plum pudding" model

J.J. Thomson, the discoverer of the electron, suggested that the arrangement of protons and electrons within an atom could be approximated by dried fruit in a plum pudding. Thomson, whose discovery of the electron preceded that of the proton or neutron, hypothesized that an atom's electrons, the dried plums, were positioned uniformly inside the atom within a cloud of positive charge, the pudding. This model was later disproved.

Rutherford scattering

Ernest Rutherford concluded from the work of Geiger and Marsden that the majority of the mass was concentrated in a minute, positively charged region, the nucleus, which was surrounded by electrons. When a positive alpha particle approached close enough to the nucleus, it was strongly

Copyright © Mometrix Media. You have been licensed one copy of this document for personal use only. Any other reproduction or redistribution is strictly prohibited. All rights reserved.

repelled, enough so that it had the ability to rebound at high angles. The small nucleus size explained the small number of alpha particles that were repelled in this fashion. The scattering led to development of the planetary model of the atom, which was further developed by Niels Bohr into what is now known as the Bohr model.

Atomic spectra dynamics

Electrons in atoms have specific allowed energy levels. They gain or lose energy by traveling between levels and absorbing or emitting photons. Zero energy is achieved in an electron that is resting at an infinite distance from the nucleus. Each type of atom has a different set of allowed energy levels. Atoms can drop from an allowed energy E2 to a lower energy level E1 by the emission of a photon with energy E, equal to the difference between E1 and E2. Additionally, the frequency of the emitted photon is equal to the energy difference divided by Planck's constant (h = 6.63×10^{-34} J-s). Similarly, an electron may move to a higher allowed energy level by absorbing an energized photon.

Bohr model

Niels Bohr postulated that the electrons orbiting the nucleus must occupy discrete orbits. These discrete orbits also corresponded to discrete levels of energy and angular momentum. Consequently, the only way that electrons could move between orbits was by making nearly instantaneous jumps between them. These jumps, known as quantum leaps, are associated with the absorption or emission of a quantum of energy, known as a photon. If the electron is jumping to a higher energy state, a photon must be absorbed. Similarly, if the electron is dropping to a lower energy state, a photon must be emitted.

Subatomic particles

The three subatomic particles are the proton, electron, and neutron. Protons are the positively charged particles in the nucleus, with a mass of 1.67252×10^{-24} g. This is approximately 1,840 times the mass of the oppositely charged electron, 9.1095×10^{-28} g. Neutrons are also present in the nucleus, are electrically neutral, and have a mass slightly greater than that of protons, 1.67497×10^{-24} g.

The electrons are attracted to the positively charged nucleus by the electrostatic or Coulomb force, which is directly proportional to the charge of the nucleus and inversely proportional to the square of the distance from the nucleus. The protons and neutrons are held together in the nucleus by the strong nuclear force. This nuclear force is known to be much stronger than the electrostatic force since the protons do not repel one another.

Absorption spectroscopy and emission spectroscopy

When an electron makes a quantum leap from one electron shell to another, a photon is either absorbed or emitted. Because the energy levels of these shells are discrete, the energy of an absorbed or emitted photon is unique to a particular pair of shells. Thus any element can be positively identified by the energy levels of the photons it emits.

Spectroscopy is most commonly used to determine the composition of unknown compounds. In absorption spectroscopy, a compound is bombarded with a full spectrum of photons, causing the compound to absorb those photons corresponding to its constituent elements' electron shell energy

Copyright © Mometrix Media. You have been licensed one copy of this document for personal use only. Any other reproduction or redistribution is strictly prohibited. All rights reserved.

levels. By capturing and measuring the wavelengths of the photons not absorbed, it can be determined which wavelengths, and thus which energy levels, were absorbed, giving the identity of the elements contained in the compound. The resulting visible spectrum consists of color from red to violet with black bands at the wavelength of the absorbed photons.

Emission spectroscopy works in a similar fashion. The compound's electrons are excited by an application of energy and allowed to decay back down to lower energy levels. This decay is necessarily accompanied by an emission of photons, whose wavelengths are measured to determine the identity of the elements. The resulting visible spectrum consists of colored bands at the wavelengths of the emitted photons.

Electron shells and the principal quantum number

Electrons around an atom are organized into what are known as orbitals or shells. These shells are located at discrete mean distances from the nucleus. A principal quantum number, denoted by the letter n, is assigned to each shell. The more distant shells have a greater capacity than those that are closer to the nucleus. The specific radii for the shells are unique to each element. The radius of the shell closest to the nucleus, n = 1, is designated r_1. The r_1 of a hydrogen atom is known as the Bohr radius and is approximately 52.9 picometers. Successive radii for the hydrogen atom's shells are found by the equation, $r_n = r_1 n^2$.

Atomic number

All atoms can be identified by the number of protons and neutrons that they contain. The atomic number, often denoted as Z, is the number of protons in the nucleus of each atom of an element. In an electrically neutral atom, the number of protons is equal to the number of electrons.

Atomic mass number

The atomic mass number, often denoted as A, is the total number of nucleons (neutrons and protons present in the nucleus) in each atom of an element.

Isotope

Atoms that have the same atomic number but different mass numbers are called isotopes. A similar term is nuclide, which refers to an atom with a given number of protons and neutrons. Atoms of a given element typically do not all have the same mass. For example, there are three hydrogen isotopes: protium, which has one proton and no neutrons; deuterium, which has one proton and one neutron; and tritium, which has one proton and two neutrons. Isotopes are denoted by the element symbol, preceded in superscript and subscript by the mass number and atomic number, respectively. For instance, the notations for protium, deuterium, and tritium are, respectively:

$$_1^1 H, \ _1^2 H, \text{ and } _1^3 H.$$

Radioactive decay and half-life

Radioactive decay, or radioactivity, is a set of processes that allow unstable atomic nuclei, or nuclides, to emit subatomic particles, or radiation. The decay is a random process and it is not possible to predict an individual atom's decay. Radioactive decay occurs at an exponential rate.

Copyright © Mometrix Media. You have been licensed one copy of this document for personal use only. Any other reproduction or redistribution is strictly prohibited. All rights reserved.

This means that the amount of radioactive material, A, present after time t is given by the equation $A = A_0 e^{kt}$, where A_0 is the amount of material present at time $t = 0$, and k is the activity of the material. The activity may be given, but it can also be determined if the amount of material present at two different times is known.

The time required for half the mass of a radioactive material to decay is known as its half-life. Half-life is the most commonly used measure of a material's rate of decay. A half-life can be as short as a fraction of a second or as long as millions of years.

Certain isotopes that are known to be unstable and spontaneously decay are referred to as radioisotopes. One common radioisotope used to determine the age of an object is carbon-14. Over time, this isotope decays to nitrogen-14. The half-life of carbon-14 is about 5,730 years.
An ordinarily stable isotope may be artificially made radioactive by bombarding it with a stream of neutrons. When these neutrons are captured by a previously stable nucleus, it can become unstable and begin to decay.

Changing energy level of an electron

An electron resting at an infinite distance from the nucleus of an atom is defined as having zero energy. When an electron is added to one of the shells surrounding an atom, it acquires negative energy. The energy level of the electron is inversely proportional to the shell's mean radius. For hydrogen, this means that the energy level is inversely proportional to the square of the shell's quantum number, $E_n = -R_H/n^2$, where R_H is the Rydberg constant, approximately 2.18×10^{-18} J. The energy gained or lost by an electron jumping from shell p to shell q in a hydrogen atom is given by $E_{pq} = R_H(1/n_p^2 - 1/n_q^2)$. This is equivalent to the energy of the photon emitted or absorbed during this electron jump. By substituting the relation between energy and photon frequency or wavelength, one can obtain equations for those two quantities as functions of the two principal quantum numbers.

The electron-binding energy of an atom is the energy required to remove all electrons from their shells. This is equivalent to moving each electron into shell $n = \infty$. For a hydrogen atom, the binding energy is equal to the Rydberg constant.

Beta decay

Beta decay is radioactive decay in which there is an emission of a beta particle, a high-energy electron or positron. For an electron emission, it is known as beta minus (β-) decay. For a positron emission, it is known as beta plus (β+) decay. In β- decay, a neutron is converted into a proton, an electron, and an antineutrino, v_e:

$$n \rightarrow p^+ + e^- + \overline{v}_e$$

This is because a down quark is converted to an up quark, emitting an electron and an antineutrino. In β+ decay, a proton is converted into a neutron by means of an up quark becoming a down quark, emitting a positron and a neutrino:

$$energy + p^+ \rightarrow n + e^+ + v_e$$

Unlike β- decay, β+ decay cannot occur spontaneously. It requires an input of energy.

Copyright © Mometrix Media. You have been licensed one copy of this document for personal use only. Any other reproduction or redistribution is strictly prohibited. All rights reserved.

In both types of beta decay, the atomic number changes, but the mass number remains constant.

Alpha decay

Alpha decay is a type of radioactive decay in which an alpha particle is ejected from the nucleus. An alpha particle is the nucleus of a helium atom, consisting of 2 protons and 2 neutrons. Ejection of an alpha particle reduces the parent nuclide's atomic number by 2 and its mass number by 4. An example of alpha decay is given by:

$$^{238}U \rightarrow {}^{234}Th + \alpha$$

Alpha decay can be looked at as nuclear fission, in which the parent nucleus splits into a pair of daughter nuclei. Alpha decay is governed by the strong nuclear force, or the force between two or more nucleons. Alpha particles are ejected from the nucleus at speeds around 15,000 km/s with a typical kinetic energy of 5 MeV.

Elementary particles

The two basic types of elementary particles are bosons, which have integer spin, and fermions, which have half-integer spin. There are a few different types of bosons, but the type most commonly encountered are photons, which make up the full spectrum of light.

There are only two types of fermions: leptons and quarks. Both leptons and quarks have antiparticles as well, with opposite charge.

Leptons may be one of three different flavors: muon, tauon, or electron. Each of these is accompanied by a small electrically neutral particle called a neutrino, also differentiated by the same three flavors. Each lepton has a charge of -1, while its antiparticle has a charge of +1. The electron's antiparticle is the positron.

Quarks are most commonly encountered as the constituent particles of nucleons. There are six different flavors of quark, of which the two most common are up, having a charge of +2/3, and down, having a charge of -1/3. Neutrons consist of one up quark and two down quarks, while protons have two up quarks and one down quark.

Gamma rays

A gamma ray (γ) is electromagnetic radiation that is produced from radioactive decay or other nuclear processes, such as electron annihilation in which an electron and positron collide. No physical difference exists between X-rays and gamma rays that have the same energy; they are set apart by their origin. Gamma rays are high-energy electromagnetic radiation that result from nuclear transitions, while X-rays are high-energy radiation caused by energy transitions from electrons that are accelerating. Gamma rays penetrate more than either alpha or beta radiation, neither of which is electromagnetic, but they are not as ionizing. Gamma sources have a wide variety of uses ranging from medical to industrial.

Copyright © Mometrix Media. You have been licensed one copy of this document for personal use only. Any other reproduction or redistribution is strictly prohibited. All rights reserved.

The basic organization of matter

An element is the most basic type of matter. It has unique properties and cannot be broken down into other elements. The smallest unit of an element is the atom. A chemical combination of two or more types of elements is called a compound. Compounds often have properties that are very different from those of their constituent elements. The smallest independent unit of an element or compound is known as a molecule. Most elements are found somewhere in nature in single-atom form, but a few elements only exist naturally in pairs. These are called diatomic elements, of which some of the most common are hydrogen, nitrogen, and oxygen. Elements and compounds are represented by chemical symbols, one or two letters, most often the first in the element name. More than one atom of the same element in a compound is represented with a subscript number designating how many atoms of that element are present. Water, for instance, contains two hydrogens and one oxygen. Thus, the chemical formula is H_2O. Methane contains one carbon and four hydrogens, so its formula is CH_4.

Ionizing and non-ionizing radiation

Electromagnetic radiation can be either ionizing radiation or non-ionizing radiation, depending on whether it is able to ionize atoms and break chemical bonds. Frequencies in the ultraviolet range and higher, such as gamma rays or X-rays, are ionizing. These have their own potential dangers. Non-ionizing radiation is not capable of having such effects on molecules, at least in this context. Three potential hazards that are considered major exist with non-ionizing electromagnetic radiation. They are electrical, biological, and fire. The induced current caused by radiation can pose significant dangers in handling pyrotechnics. Induced current can cause electric shock to humans or animals. A strong electromagnetic field may cause electric currents that can flow over air gaps to the ground, causing sparks and fire. The biological hazard stems from electromagnetic fields causing dielectric heating and can lead to tissue and other bodily damage.

Mixtures with compounds

Mixtures are similar to compounds in that they are produced when two or more substances are combined. However, there are some key differences as well. Compounds require a chemical combination of the constituent particles, while mixtures are simply the interspersion of particles. Unlike compounds, mixtures may be separated without a chemical change. A mixture retains the chemical properties of its constitutent particles, while a compound acquires a new set of properties. Given compounds can exist only in specific ratios, while mixtures may be any ratio of the involved substances.

Mixture, colloid, solution, and concentration

A mixture is made of two or more substances that are combined in various proportions with each retaining its own specific properties. A mixture's components may be separated by physical means: that is, without making and breaking chemical bonds. An example would be table salt being completely dissolved in water. Heterogeneous mixtures are those in which the composition and properties are not uniform throughout the entire sample. Examples include concrete and wood. A colloid is a special type of mixture in which small particles are suspended, but not dissolved, in a liquid. Homogeneous mixtures are those in which the composition and properties are uniform throughout the entire sample. This type of mixture is also known as a solution. If there is only one liquid present in the solution, that liquid is referred to as the solvent and the remaining substances

Copyright © Mometrix Media. You have been licensed one copy of this document for personal use only. Any other reproduction or redistribution is strictly prohibited. All rights reserved.

are the solutes. If there are multiple liquids, the most prevalent is considered the solvent. Solutions consisting primarily of water are referred to as aqueous solutions. The concentration of a solution is the ratio of solute present, often given as mass of solute per volume of solution. A solution with low concentration is referred to as dilute.

Six different types of phase change

A substance that is undergoing a change from a solid to a liquid is said to be melting. If this change occurs in the opposite direction, from liquid to solid, this change is called freezing. A liquid which is being converted to a gas is undergoing vaporization. The reverse of this process is known as condensation. Direct transitions from gas to solid and solid to gas are much less common in everyday life, but they can occur given the proper conditions. Solid to gas conversion is known as sublimation, while the reverse is called deposition.

Three states of matter

The three states in which matter can exist are solid, liquid, and gas. They differ from each other in the motion of and attraction between individual molecules. In a solid, the molecules have little or no motion and are heavily attracted to neighboring molecules, giving them a definite structure. This structure may be ordered/crystalline or random/amorphous. Liquids also have considerable attraction between molecules, but the molecules are much more mobile, having no set structure. In a gas, the molecules have little or no attraction to one another and are constantly in motion. They are separated by distances that are very large in comparison to the size of the molecules. Gases easily expand to fill whatever space is available. Unlike solids and liquids, gases are easily compressible.

The three states of matter can be traversed by the addition or removal of heat. For example, when a solid is heated to its melting point, it can begin to form a liquid. However, in order to transition from solid to liquid, additional heat must be added at the melting point to overcome the latent heat of fusion. Upon further heating to its boiling point, the liquid can begin to form a gas, but again, additional heat must be added at the boiling point to overcome the latent heat of vaporization.

Nuclear binding energy

The nuclear binding energy of an atom is the energy that would be required to disassemble the nucleus into its constituent nucleons. They are held together by a strong nuclear force in the nucleus. Nuclear binding energy may be calculated by determining the difference in mass between the nucleus and the sum of the masses of its constituent particles. This mass, m, is converted to energy by the equation $E = mc^2$, where c is the speed of light in a vacuum.

Nuclei may be transformed by a rearrangement of nucleons. These nuclear transformations may occur by many different means, including radioactive decay, nuclear fusion, and nuclear fission. In nuclear fusion, two light nuclei merge into a single nucleus that is heavier. In nuclear fission, a single large nucleus divides into two or more smaller nuclei. In either case, if the mass of the nuclei before transformation is greater than the mass after transformation, then it is an exothermic process. Conversely, if the mass is greater after transformation, the process is endothermic. Nickel and iron have the most stable nuclei of any elements, having the largest binding energies.

Copyright © Mometrix Media. You have been licensed one copy of this document for personal use only. Any other reproduction or redistribution is strictly prohibited. All rights reserved.

Plasma

Plasma is an ionized gas. However, its properties are different enough from common gas that it is classified as a separate state of matter. It is a gas in which enough energy is provided to free some of the electrons from their atoms. This allows both ions and electrons to coexist. Plasma can be viewed as a cloud of protons, neutrons, and electrons. This enables the plasma to act as a whole rather than as a conglomerate of atoms. This also makes plasma highly electrically conductive and easily affected by electromagnetic fields. More than 99 percent of the visible universe is made up of plasma, making it the most common state of matter. Plasma is naturally occurring. It is what makes up the sun and the core of stars, and is also found in quasars.

Conservation laws that apply to nuclear reactions

In nuclear reactions, neither mass nor energy is fully conserved independently. However, the mass-energy relation is conserved. Any mass loss is converted to energy and any energy loss is converted to mass, both by the equation $E = mc^2$, where c is the speed of light in a vacuum. Generally speaking, however, there will not be a significant loss of mass in a reaction and the total number of protons and neutrons will be constant. Additionally, electric charge is conserved in nuclear reactions. For instance, when an alpha particle is ejected, it reduces the charge of the parent nucleus by 2, and itself carries a charge of +2. In beta plus decay, a proton decays to a neutron, reducing the charge of the atom by 1, but a positron with a charge of +1 is also ejected, conserving charge in the reaction. Similarly, in beta minus decay, a neutron is converted to a proton, increasing the atom's charge by 1, but this is accompanied by the ejection of an electron with a charge of -1.

Unknown products in a nuclear reaction can be predicted by balancing those quantities which must be conserved. For instance, if it is known that plutonium-238 decays to cesium-140 upon being impacted by a neutron, ejecting 2 more neutrons in the process, the remaining products may be determined. Since there are no charged particles emitted, the number of protons must remain constant. Of the 94 protons in plutonium, 55 form the cesium atom, leaving 39 protons to form an yttrium atom. Since the number of neutrons must also be constant, this will be an atom of yttrium-97.

Fusion and fission

Fusion generally requires a large input of energy to overcome the repulsive force between nuclei, but after transformation it produces an even greater amount of energy. This makes fusion reactions difficult to control, so fission is generally chosen over fusion for power-generation applications. The energy and radiation given off by stars are the product of countless fusion chain reactions.

Fission is most often initiated by bombarding atoms with a stream of neutrons, destabilizing the atoms and causing a fission into smaller nuclei and emission of numerous radiation particles, including more neutrons, thus perpetuating the reaction. These reactions are easily sustainable and much more easily controlled than fusion, so they are ideal for generating power. However, a fission reaction can be initiated that does not propagate in a controlled manner. This type of reaction is commonly used in nuclear weapons.

Copyright © Mometrix Media. You have been licensed one copy of this document for personal use only. Any other reproduction or redistribution is strictly prohibited. All rights reserved.

Photoelectric effect

The photoelectric effect is the emission of electrons by substances when light falls on their surfaces. One of the main inspirations for the development of quantum theory was the inability of the standard theory of electromagnetic radiation to fully explain the photoelectric effect. Einstein declared that the incident light is composed of discrete particles of energy, known as quanta. The quanta of energy in light are known as photons. The energy of each photon is proportional to its frequency according to the equation $E = hf$, where E is energy, h is Planck's constant, and f is the frequency. When light is incident on a portion of an electric circuit, a current may be induced in the circuit. One property associated with this effect is stopping potential. This value is dependent on both the surface metal and the frequency of the incident light. Light of a given frequency will induce a current only if it does not have to overcome more potential in the circuit than the stopping potential. The stopping potential, V_0, is calculated by the equation $eV_0 = hf - \varphi$, where e is the elementary charge and φ is the work function of the metal. If $hf - \varphi$ is calculated in electron volts, V_0 is simply the equivalent number of volts.

Blackbody radiation

A *black body* is an ideal black substance that will absorb all and reflect none of the radiation energy that falls on it. Powdered carbon is the closest real approximation of a black body. Because a black body is a perfect absorber of radiation, it is also a perfect emitter of radiation. The distribution of radiant energy in a black body according to wavelength will depend on the absolute temperature of the body: the higher the temperature, the lower the wavelength at which energy is distributed as a maximum. Blackbody radiation was used by Max Planck to develop the quantum theory of mechanics in 1901.

Heisenberg uncertainty principle

Wave-particle duality is the insight of quantum mechanics that states that energy will behave with the characteristics of both a particle and a wave. For most of the history of physics, it was believed that light was composed of electromagnetic waves and electrons were tiny particles of matter. However, experiments with light have created situations in which light will behave as if it were a particle (called a *photon*), and other experiments have suggested that photons will often behave as if they were waves. Quantum mechanics was essentially created to resolve this conundrum. The result has been a series of theories, including the de Broglie hypothesis, that try to unify these seemingly contradictory attributes of matter.

One important measurement issue that arises from this dual nature is the Heisenberg uncertainty principle. This principle states that the position and linear momentum cannot be accurately measured beyond a certain level. Specifically, the minimum uncertainty in measuring the position, x, and linear momentum, p, in a given dimension is dictated by the relation $(\Delta x)(\Delta p) \geq h/4pi$, where h is Planck's constant.

De Broglie's hypothesis

The de Broglie hypothesis is the assertion that all matter has a wave-like nature. It is not just subatomic particles that exhibit wave properties; all objects do. This insight of de Broglie was confirmed by experiments that fired electrons at a very high speed at a crystalline nickel target. The diffraction of the electrons upon impacting the target was consistent with the diffraction

Copyright © Mometrix Media. You have been licensed one copy of this document for personal use only. Any other reproduction or redistribution is strictly prohibited. All rights reserved.

exhibited by waves when passing through a slit with a width approximately the same as the wavelength of the wave. From these experiments, he produced two relations for an electron's frequency, f, and wavelength, λ, similar to those for photons: $f = E/h$ and $\lambda = h/p$, where E is the electron's energy, p is its linear momentum, and h is Planck's constant.

Michelson-Morley experiment

The Michelson-Morley experiment proved that there is no substance like ether in outer space. It involved the use of a Michelson interferometer, a device that measures length to a great degree of precision by means of interference fringes. Basically, an interferometer sends two beams of light out, splits them at right angles to one another, and then brings them back to a central location with a mirror. Any very minor shift in the position of the beams will be seen as a shift in the interference fringes. Michelson and Morley wanted to use this device to determine the characteristics of the ether wind that blew through outer space and affected the transmission of light, but instead they ended up disproving the existence of the ether altogether. They were also able to conclude from this experiment that the measured velocity of light is independent of the observer's reference-frame velocity.

Einstein's theory of relativity

Relativity is composed of special relativity and general relativity. Special relativity relates that those observers in inertial reference frames, in uniform motion relative to each other, cannot perform experiments to find out which is stationary. This is the principle of relativity, which says that regardless of an observer's velocity or position in the universe, all physical laws will appear constant. It was in this context that Einstein found that the speed of light in a vacuum had to be the same for all the observers despite their motion or the motion of the light source. General relativity is a geometrical theory that reasons that the presence of mass and energy will curve space-time, a model that combines to form the space-time continuum, and that the curvature will affect the path of free particles. This includes the path of light. It uses differential geometry and the generalized quantity of tensors to describe gravitation without using the force of gravity. The theory postulates that all observers should be equivalent, not only those that move with uniform speed.

Lorentz transformations and equations

Because of the phenomena associated with Einstein's theory of relativity, measurements taken from reference frames traveling at high velocities may noticeably differ from those taken in a stationary reference frame. These differences in observation may be reconciled using Lorentz transformations. In the equations that follow, all quantities with a subscript zero represent those quantities as measured in a stationary frame. The primary conversion factor in these equations is the Lorentz factor, $\gamma = 1/\text{sqrt}(1 - v^2/c^2)$. The equations for Lorentz contraction and time dilation both use this factor.
$L = L_0/\gamma$, where L is the observed length of an object in the direction of the frame's velocity. As observed from a high-velocity frame, objects will appear shorter.

Also, $\Delta t = \Delta t_0 \gamma$, where Δt is elapsed time in a stationary frame as observed from a high-velocity frame. This means that from the high-velocity frame, time will seem to pass more quickly in the stationary frame.

One further equation relating high-velocity and stationary-frame measurements is velocity addition. For those velocities encountered in everyday life, an observer traveling at velocity, v, who

- 34 -

Copyright © Mometrix Media. You have been licensed one copy of this document for personal use only. Any other reproduction or redistribution is strictly prohibited. All rights reserved.

measures an object's velocity as u', traveling in the same direction, will reasonably assume that the object's velocity in a stationary frame is u = v + u'. For velocities significant relative to the speed of light, c, the equation becomes u = (v + u')/(1 + vu'/c²).

Simultaneous events

Let us imagine a situation in which one stationary observer records two events that happen at the same time. If another observer moving at a constant velocity also records these two events, it is unlikely that the moving observer will record these two events as having happened simultaneously. In other words, two observers who are in relative motion will not generally agree as to whether two events are simultaneous. Neither observer is objectively right or wrong. We may therefore conclude that simultaneity is not an absolute concept but a relative one. It depends on the state of motion of the observer. Of course, since in most cases the speed of the observers will be a great deal less than the speed of light, this lack of simultaneity will be too small to notice.

Copyright © Mometrix Media. You have been licensed one copy of this document for personal use only. Any other reproduction or redistribution is strictly prohibited. All rights reserved.

Electricity and Magnetism

Electric field equation

In order to define a particular electric field, we may place an object with positive charge, q_0, called a test charge, somewhere near the charged particle, and then measure the force exerted on the object. We may then say that electric field E at that point is $E = F/q_0$. Electric field is a vector, and the direction of E will be the direction of the force acting on the test charge. If we want to fully define some region of an electric field, we must find measures for electric field at every point within that region. The SI units for electric field are Newtons per coulomb. When performing this operation, we will assume that the presence of the test charge does not affect in any way the charge distribution of the electric field.

Coulomb's law

If two particles have charge magnitudes q_1 and q_2, and are separated by distance r, then the electrostatic force of attraction or repulsion between them can be calculated as $F = kq_1q_2/r^2$, in which k is a constant, approximately 9×10^9 N-m^2/C^2. This is known as Coulomb's law. We should note the similarity to Newton's equation for the gravitational force between two particles, $F = Gm_1m_2/r^2$. The main difference between these two equations is that while electrical force may be attractive or repulsive, gravitational force is always attractive. No experiment has ever contradicted Coulomb's law, even those conducted at the subatomic level. The constant k in the equation is called Coulomb's constant or the electrostatic constant. An important principle when calculating electrostatic force, if more than two particles are involved, is the law of superposition. If we are looking for the force exerted on a particle by two or more other particles, we must determine the individual force from each of the other particles, and take the vector sum of those forces to determine the total effect.

Gauss's Law

Flux is a concept that is applicable in many areas of science. It is a measure of flow through a given area. Electric flux, Φ, is a measure of the electric field flowing perpendicularly through a particular area. It can be calculated by the equation $\Phi = E \cdot A = EA\cos(\theta)$, where θ is the angle between the direction of E and the normal vector of A.

Gauss's law states that the electric flux through an enclosing surface is directly related to charge enclosed by the surface. This relation is given by the equation $\Phi = Q/\varepsilon_0$, where ε_0 is a constant known as the permittivity of free space. The shape of the enclosing surface should be chosen to accommodate the finding of E·A. Most often, this will be a sphere or cylinder, since these surfaces are perpendicular to field lines emanating from a point or line charge, respectively. Combining the two equations yields the relation, $Q/\varepsilon_0 = E \cdot A$. Units for electric flux are N-m^2/C.

Electric potential

Electric potential energy is the energy stored in a charge by virtue of its proximity to other charged regions. It can be calculated in the same way as calculating the amount of work required to move it to that location from an infinite distance away. The work required to move a charge of magnitude q

Copyright © Mometrix Media. You have been licensed one copy of this document for personal use only. Any other reproduction or redistribution is strictly prohibited. All rights reserved.

from infinity to a distance r from another charge of magnitude Q is calculated to be $PE_e = W = kQq/r$, where k is the electrostatic constant.

Electric potential, V, is closely related to electric potential energy. The potential due to a charge Q can be found by dividing the electric potential energy of another charge q by its magnitude, $V = PE_e/q$, or by the equation $V = kQ/r$.

The difference between the electric potential of two points is known as voltage. It is measured in volts, or joules per coulomb. Since it is impractical to find a point of zero absolute electric potential, for each system a reference point or ground is defined, to which all other points in the system may be related.

Common means of transferring electrical charge

Charge is transferred in three common ways: conduction, induction, and friction. Conduction, as the name implies, takes place between conductive materials. There must be a point of contact between the two materials and a potential difference, such as when a battery is connected to a circuit. Induction also requires conductive materials. It occurs due to one material encountering a varying magnetic field. This can be the result of a changing magnetic field or the material moving within a constant magnetic field. Charge transfer due to friction does not require conductive materials. When two materials are rubbed together, electrons may be transferred from one to the other, leaving the two materials with equal and opposite charges. This is observed when shoes are dragged across a carpeted floor.

Conductors, insulators, and semiconductors

In many materials, electrons are able to move freely; these are known as conductors. Due to their atomic structure and delocalized electrons, metals tend to be the best conductors, particularly copper and silver. Highly conductive wires are instrumental in creating low-resistance pathways for electrons to travel along within a circuit.

Other materials naturally inhibit the movement of charge and are known as insulators. Their electrons are tightly held by the individual constituent atoms. Glass, pure water, wood, and plastic are all insulators. Insulators are necessary in circuits to prevent charge from escaping to undesirable places, such as an operator's hand. For this reason, most highly conductive materials are covered by insulators.

Semiconductors, as the name suggests, are materials that only partially conduct electrical charge. The elements silicon and germanium are both common semiconductors, and are frequently used in microelectronic devices because they allow for tight control of the rate of conduction. In many cases, the conduction ability of semiconductors can be controlled by adjusting the temperature of the material.

Electromotive force and common EMF devices

A force that maintains a potential difference between two locations in a circuit is known as an electromotive force. A device that creates this force is referred to as an EMF device. The most common EMF device is the battery. Batteries operate by converting chemical energy stored in the electrolyte, the internal chemical material, into electrical energy. The reaction causes an abundance of electrons on the cathode, and when the circuit is connected, they flow to the anode, creating a flow of current. The electrolyte's composition also determines whether the battery is classified as

Copyright © Mometrix Media. You have been licensed one copy of this document for personal use only. Any other reproduction or redistribution is strictly prohibited. All rights reserved.

acidic or alkaline, and wet or dry. Another EMF device is the photocell, also commonly called the solar cell, since most photocells are powered by the sun. These operate by absorbing photons, which cause the electrons to be excited and flow in a current, a process of converting light energy into electrical energy. A third type of EMF device is the generator. This device converts mechanical energy to electrical energy. A generator may be powered by such diverse sources as gasoline engines, flowing water, or even manually powered cranks. These devices utilize a rotating shaft to spin a coil within a magnetic field, creating a potential difference by induction.

Capacitors and dielectrics

Capacitors are devices used in circuits to store energy in the form of electric fields. They are most often composed of two oppositely charged parallel plates separated by a medium, generally air. This medium is referred to as the capacitor's dielectric. The dielectric material dictates the amount of energy in the electric field and, consequently, the amount of energy that can be stored by the capacitor. The measurable quality of a capacitor is known as its capacitance, or the amount of charge that it can store per volt of potential difference. This is given by the equation $C = Q/V$, with capacitance having units of farads or coulombs per volt. Physically, the capacitance depends on three things: the area of the parallel plates, the separation distance between them, and the dielectric material. For cases in which the separation distance is insignificant compared to the area, the capacitance can be found by the equation $C = \varepsilon A/d$, where ε is the permittivity of the dielectric material. Often, instead of being given the permittivity, we will be given the dielectric constant, κ, which is the ratio of the permittivities of the material and air, $\kappa = \varepsilon/\varepsilon_{air}$. This yields an obvious result of $\kappa_{air} = 1$.

The energy stored in a capacitor can be calculated in three different ways: $E = CV^2/2 = Q^2/2C = VQ/2$. Another quantity associated with capacitors is the electric field energy density, η. This energy density is found by $\eta = \varepsilon E^2/2$.

Ohm's Law

If we were to apply the exact same potential difference between the ends of two geometrically similar rods, one made of copper and one made of glass, we would create vastly different currents. This is because these two substances have different resistances. Ohm's Law describes the relation between applied voltage and induced current, $V = IR$. This is one of the most important tools of circuit analysis. Resistance, then, can be calculated as $R = V/I$. The SI unit for resistance is the ohm (Ω), equal to a volt per ampere. When a conductor is placed into a circuit to provide a specific resistance, it is known as a resistor. For a given potential difference, the greater the resistance is to the current, the smaller the current will be.

If we wish to look instead at the quality of the material of which the resistor is made, then we must consider resistivity. Resistivity, ρ, is a physical property of every material, which, if known, can be used to size a resistor for a specific resistance. Resistance is dictated by both the material and the dimensions of the resistor, given by the relation $R = \rho L/A$, where L is the effective length of the resistor and A is the effective cross-section. Alternatively, an unknown resistivity may be calculated by rearranging the equation as $\rho = RA/L$.

The resistivity will often change with temperature. In these cases, the relevant resistivity may be calculated $\rho = \rho_{ref}(1 + \alpha(T - T_{ref}))$, where α is the resistivity proportionality constant and T is the material temperature.

Copyright © Mometrix Media. You have been licensed one copy of this document for personal use only. Any other reproduction or redistribution is strictly prohibited. All rights reserved.

Electric current

An electric current is simply an electric charge in motion. Electric current cannot exist unless there is a difference in electric potential. If, for instance, we have an isolated conducting loop, it will be at the same potential throughout. If, however, we insert a battery into this loop, then the conducting loop will no longer be at a single electric potential. A flow of electrons will result and will very quickly reach a steady state. At that point, it will be completely analogous to steady-state fluid flow. A current is quantified by the amount of charge that is transferred in a given amount of time. The SI unit for current is the ampere (A), equal to a coulomb of charge per second.

Capacitors and inductors in AC circuits

Because of the constantly fluctuating nature of alternating current, capacitors and inductors both oppose immediate acceptance of the fluctuation. This opposition is referred to as impedance and is similar to resistance, also having units of ohms, but unlike resistance, impedance is a complex value, meaning that it may have an imaginary component as well as a real component. For ideal capacitors and inductors, impedance is purely imaginary, and for ideal resistors, impedance is purely real. It is only when combining the effects of these devices that the full expression for impedance, Z, is necessary: $Z = R + Xi$, where $i = sqrt(-1)$. X is a quantity known as reactance. For capacitors, $X_C = 1/\omega C$, where ω is the angular frequency of the current, and for inductors, $X_L = \omega L$.

The use of Ohm's Law and Kirchhoff's laws

Circuit analysis is the process of determining the current or voltage drop across devices of interest in a circuit. Ohm's Law is useful in doing this since it definitively relates the current to the voltage drop for resistors, $V = IR$. Kirchhoff's voltage law (KVL) states that if you sum the voltage drops across all devices in any closed loop of a circuit, the sum will always be zero, $V_1 + V_2 + ... + V_n = 0$. This law is particularly useful if there are multiple closed-loop pathways in a circuit. Kirchhoff's current law (KCL) states that the amount of current entering a point must equal the amount of current leaving, $I_{in} = I_{out}$. This law may also be expanded to apply to the current entering and leaving a larger region of a circuit. In any given circuit analysis, it may be necessary to use all three of these laws.

Another important principle to remember in an ideal circuit is that any two points connected by only wire are at equal voltage. Only devices on the circuit may change the voltage. In actual practice, however, all wire has some amount of resistance. A battery that provides an EMF of V_B is only able to deliver a voltage to the circuit of $V = V_B - IR_B$, where R_B is the internal resistance of the battery. To express this concept in an ideal circuit, we would need to add a small resistor in series after the battery.

Energy and power

Electric circuits operate by transferring electrical energy from one location in the circuit to another. Some devices in a circuit can store and release energy while other devices, like resistors, simply dissipate energy. Power is a measure of the rate at which energy is stored, released, transferred, or dissipated. It is measured in watts (W), or joules per second. Power is calculated by $P = VI$. The amount of power being released by a 9-V battery producing a current of 5 A is 45 W. When calculating the amount of power dissipated by a resistor, Ohm's Law allows two other equations for power, $P = I^2R = V^2/R$.

Copyright © Mometrix Media. You have been licensed one copy of this document for personal use only. Any other reproduction or redistribution is strictly prohibited. All rights reserved.

When power consumption over long periods of time needs to be measured, it will often be measured in units of kilowatt-hours, which is the amount of energy consumed at a rate of 1 kW over the course of an hour. One kilowatt-hour is equal to 3600 kJ.

RC circuits

An RC circuit consists of a battery wired in series with a resistor and a capacitor. Since a capacitor in steady state allows no current flow, it makes no sense to analyze a steady-state RC circuit. Instead, we will look at an RC circuit that has only just been connected, with the capacitor uncharged. The battery supplies voltage V_B to the circuit, and since the capacitor's voltage is initially zero, the voltage across the resistor is initially V_B, giving an initial current of $I = V_B/R$. As current flows, the charge on the capacitor increases, which in turn creates an opposing voltage that lowers the voltage drop across the resistor. Combining Ohm's Law with the KVL gives the voltage relation as $V_B = IR + Q/C$, where Q is the charge on the capacitor. Since the current is simply the transfer rate of the charge, this becomes a differential equation. Solving for charge and current yields the expressions $Q(t) = CV_B(1 - e^{-t/RC})$ and $I(t) = (V_B/R)e^{-t/RC}$. The factor RC in the exponential is referred to as the circuit's time constant. It is the amount of time required for the capacitor to charge up to 63.2% capacity.

If the battery is removed from the circuit after the capacitor is charged and the circuit is reconnected with just the resistor and capacitor, the capacitor will begin to drain at the same rate that it was charged. The current magnitude will follow the same equation as before, though it will be in the opposite direction. The new expression for the charge will be $Q(t) = CV_B e^{-t/RC}$.

Circuit analysis

When resistors in a simple circuit are arranged in series with a battery, current must pass through each resistor consecutively in order to return to the battery. This immediately tells us that the current through each resistor is the same. By KVL, we know that the sum of the voltage drop across the resistors is equal to the voltage input by the battery, $V_B = IR_1 + IR_2 + ... + IR_n$. This may be restated as $V_B = I(R_1 + R_2 + ... + R_n)$. From this we can see that for resistors arranged in series, the equivalent resistance is the sum of the resistances, $R_{eq} = R_1 + R_2 + ... + R_n$.

When resistors in a simple circuit are arranged in parallel with a battery, the current need only pass through one of them to return to the battery. By KVL, we know that the voltage drop across each resistor is the same. Since the total current must equal the sum of the currents through the resistors, we may conclude from Ohm's Law that $I = V_B/R_1 + V_B/R_2 + ... + V_B/R_n$. We may restate this relation as $I = V_B(1/R_1 + 1/R_2 + ... + 1/R_n)$. Moving the resistance expression to the other side of the equation shows us that the equivalent resistance is $R_{eq} = (1/R_1 + 1/R_2 + ... + 1/R_n)^{-1}$ for resistors in parallel.

Capacitors have opposite combination rules. Capacitors in series have an equivalent value of $C_{eq} = (1/C_1 + 1/C_2 + ... + 1/C_n)^{-1}$, while capacitors in parallel have equivalence of $C_{eq} = C_1 + C_2 + ... + C_n$. Inductors follow the same rules as resistors.

Measuring Devices

There are several devices that allow these circuit quantities to be measured to a great degree of accuracy. An ammeter is a device placed in series with a circuit to measure the current through that location. Ideally, an ammeter has as little internal resistance as possible to prevent altering the

Copyright © Mometrix Media. You have been licensed one copy of this document for personal use only. Any other reproduction or redistribution is strictly prohibited. All rights reserved.

current it is trying to measure. A voltmeter measures the voltage or potential difference between two locations in a circuit. It has two leads that are connected in parallel with the circuit and consists of a very high resistance and an ammeter in series. This allows only a very small amount of current to be diverted through the voltmeter, but enough to determine the voltage by Ohm's Law. A galvanometer is the primary working component of an ammeter. It operates based on the idea that a wire in a magnetic field will experience a force proportional to the amount of current it is carrying. It converts the observed current into a dial reading. A potentiometer is a variable resistor, often controlled by a knob, that allows an operator to control the amount of voltage or current provided to a given circuit. They are commonly used in volume-control knobs. Potentiometers can also be called voltage dividers. Their use in circuit measurement is for finding voltages by comparing them to known voltages. A multimeter is a device that combines the functions of all the above devices into one. In addition to voltage, current, resistance and capacitance, they can typically measure inductance, frequency, and other quantities.

Power in AC circuits

Unlike DC circuits, the power provided by an AC voltage source is not constant over time. Generally, an AC source will provide voltage in a sinusoidal pattern, $V(t) = V_{max}\sin(\omega t)$. Similarly, the current will be given by $I(t) = I_{max}\sin(\omega t)$. From our known equations for power, this yields a power of $P(t) = RI_{max}^2\sin^2(\omega t)$. However, if we wish to find the average power or the amount of energy transmission after a given period of time, we need to find some way to average voltage and current. The root-mean-square (rms) method, as the name suggests, takes the square root of the time average of the squared value. For sinusoidal functions such as the voltage and current here, the rms value is the maximum value divided by the square root of 2. For voltage and current, $V_{rms} = V_{max}/\text{sqrt}(2)$, and $I_{rms} = I_{max}/\text{sqrt}(2)$. In this way, the average power can be found as $P_{av} = V_{rms}I_{rms}$, which can also be stated $P_{av} = V_{max}I_{max}/2$. A DC source with supplied voltage V_B will provide the same power over time as an AC source if $V_B = V_{rms}$.

Magnetic field

Magnetism and magnetic attraction are similar in many ways to electrical charge and electrostatic force. Magnets have two distinct polarities, of which like polarities repel and opposite polarities attract. Just as an object that holds an electric charge will produce a vector field, so will a charged magnet. Like the electric field lines, magnetic field lines are drawn as originating from north poles and terminating on south poles. Magnetic field is typically represented with the letter **B**, and has SI units of teslas (T), which are equivalent to N/A-m. Unlike electric charge, however, an isolated magnetic pole cannot exist. Magnets must exist as dipoles, meaning that if there is a north pole, the other end of the magnet, no matter how small, will be a south pole. Most common magnets can be demagnetized simply by heating the material or subjecting it to repeated impact. This is because magnets are composed of many tiny dipoles that, when aligned, create a large unified magnet. Some materials are permanently aligned in the manner and are known as permanent magnets. Ferromagnets are iron-based materials that can be magnetized if their dipoles are aligned by a sufficiently strong magnetic field.

Magnetic and electric fields are quite interrelated. It is believed that magnetic fields are set up by electric currents, and it has also been observed that magnetic fields can induce electric current. If we were to place a moving charge or a wire carrying current into a magnetic field, a magnetic force would act on it.

Copyright © Mometrix Media. You have been licensed one copy of this document for personal use only. Any other reproduction or redistribution is strictly prohibited. All rights reserved.

Forces exerted by a magnetic field

We will define **B**, the magnetic field, by measuring the magnetic force exerted on a moving electric charge within the field. This is generally done by firing a test charge into the area where B is to be defined. After a time, we will find that force F_B acting on a test charge of velocity **v** and charge q can be written $F_B = q\mathbf{v} \times \mathbf{B}$, in which q can be either positive or negative. If q is negative, the direction of the force will be opposite to that shown by the right-hand rule from this cross product. From this equation, we will discover that the magnetic force always acts perpendicular to the velocity vector. This means a magnetic field can neither speed up nor slow down a charged particle; it can only deflect it. Also, a magnetic field will exert no force on a stationary charge or a charge that moves parallel to the field. We can see from this equation that the magnitude of the deflecting force will be $F_B = qvBsin(\varphi)$, where φ is the angle between the particle velocity vector and the magnetic field vector.

Cyclotrons and mass spectrometers

Cyclotrons are particle accelerators that operate by using a magnetic field to create a deflection force on a fast-moving charged particle. The field strength is designed to cause the particle to move in a circular pattern. An electric field provides a force for the particle to accelerate tangentially as well. Once the particle has achieved sufficient velocity, it will exit the magnetic field and continue on in a straight line. One big advantage of the cyclotron over other types of particle accelerators is its relatively small size. Particles can achieve incredible velocities without having to travel a great distance.

Mass spectrometers are used to find the charge-to-mass ratio of ionized materials. An ionized particle of known mass, but unknown charge, is sent at a known velocity into a perpendicular magnetic field of known magnitude. Since the magnetic field is perpendicular, the tangential speed of the particle is constant. The force on a particle with constant tangential speed is equal to mv^2/r, where r is the radius of curvature of the particle's path. The force exerted by the magnetic field can be calculated as qvB, since it is perpendicular to the particle's direction of motion. Equating these two expressions gives us $q/m = v/rB$, allowing us to find the charge-to-mass ratio if we measure the radius of curvature.

Lorentz Force Law

The Lorentz force law describes the force exerted on a charged particle in an electromagnetic field. The force exerted on the particle with charge q can be found $F = q(\mathbf{E} + \mathbf{v} \times \mathbf{B})$, where **v** is the particle's velocity vector and **E** and **B** are the electric and magnetic field vectors, respectively. Essentially, this law states that a positively charged particle will be accelerated in the same linear direction as the electric field, but will curve perpendicularly to the magnetic field according to the right-hand rule. The Lorentz force law is used in a number of devices currently employed by physicists, like the cyclotron, magnetron, mass spectrometer, motor, generator, and rail gun.

Gauss's Law

Gauss's law for magnetism solidifies the assertion that magnetic monopoles cannot exist. It does so by making statements about magnetic flux, which is defined in much the same way as electric flux, $\Phi_m = \mathbf{B} \cdot \mathbf{A}$, where **A** is the surface's normal vector. Magnetic flux has SI units of webers (Wb). If the surface is taken to be an enclosing surface, or a Gaussian surface, Gauss's law states that the total flux through the surface will equal zero. Unlike the case with electric flux, which allows for

- 42 -

Copyright © Mometrix Media. You have been licensed one copy of this document for personal use only. Any other reproduction or redistribution is strictly prohibited. All rights reserved.

contained net charge, there can be no net magnetic poles inside of a closed surface. For every north pole, there must be a south pole of equal magnitude. If, for instance, we envision our Gaussian surface as enclosing one end of a short solenoid (which will set up a magnetic field resembling that of a magnetic dipole), we will notice that the magnetic field B will enter the Gaussian surface inside the solenoid (at the north pole) and will leave it outside the solenoid. No lines will begin or end in the interior of the surface, so the total flux for the surface is zero.

Magnetic force on a current-carrying wire

A magnetic field will exert a sideways force on the conduction electrons in a wire. Since the conduction electrons cannot escape sideways out of the wire, we know that this force must be transmitted bodily to the wire itself. For instance, if we have a wire carrying current I, and we know that the longitudinal axis of the wire is perpendicular to a magnetic field **B**, then we know that a force equal to (-e)vB will act on each conduction electron. Taken as a whole, the wire will experience a force of ILB, where L is the length of wire in the field. If we were to reverse either the magnetic field or the direction of the current, then the force on the wire would reverse as well. If the magnetic field is not perpendicular to the wire, then we can find the magnetic force as F_B = ILBsin(φ), where φ is the angle between the direction of current and the magnetic field vector. The torque on a current-carrying loop is a result of the same phenomenon, except that with a loop, the current travels in opposite directions on opposite sides of the loop. This causes a result of zero net force since all the current exits the field from the same direction that it entered. There is, however, a net torque since the current going in opposite directions is separated by a distance. The torque can be found by τ = IA**n**×**B**, where A is the area enclosed by the loop and **n** is the unit vector perpendicular to the plane of the loop. The loop may be any shape so long as it does not cross itself and is a closed shape.

Ampere's law

Ampere's law is described by the closed-loop line integral:
$$\oint_C B \cdot dL = \mu_0 I$$

For a straight length of wire, the magnetic field simply encircles the wire in the direction indicated by the right-hand rule (with the thumb pointed in the direction of current and the fingers curling to indicate the magnetic field). For a very long wire where end effects may be ignored, the magnetic field is given as B = μ_0I/(2pi*r), where r is the distance from the wire.

For a loop of current-carrying wire, the magnetic field direction can still be determined from the right-hand rule. However, the field magnitude at most points around and inside the loop is difficult to determine. The field magnitude at the center of the loop is found to be B = μ_0I/2r.

For a solenoid, a long coil of current-carrying wire that is sometimes wrapped around a metal core, the magnetic field direction may again be determined by the right-hand rule. At all points inside the solenoid, the field has magnitude B = μ_0nI/h, where n is the number of loops in the solenoid and h is its height. For a long solenoid, it can be shown that the field magnitude outside the solenoid is negligible.

Copyright © Mometrix Media. You have been licensed one copy of this document for personal use only. Any other reproduction or redistribution is strictly prohibited. All rights reserved.

Biot-Savart law

Any current-carrying wire will produce a magnetic field that circles the wire in the direction indicated by the right-hand rule (with the thumb pointing in the direction of the current). The Biot-Savart law gives the magnitude and direction of the magnetic field created by each infinitesimal element of current. The equation form of this law is given as $d\mathbf{B} = (\mu_0 I/4r^3 pi)*d\mathbf{L} \times \mathbf{r}$, where μ_0 is a physical constant called the permeability of free space, $d\mathbf{L}$ is an infinitesimal vector pointing along the length of the wire in the direction of current, and $\mathbf{r}$ is the vector pointing from the wire element to the location where the field is to be calculated. Integrating this expression along the full length of wire gives the total resultant field. Ampere's law states this concept in the form of a closed-loop line integral:

$$\oint_C B \cdot dL = \mu_0 I$$

The primary shortcoming of Ampere's law is that it is only applicable for a constant steady-state current. For transient cases, such as RC circuits, it is necessary to take into account what is known as the displacement current. Displacement current is found by the equation $I_d = \varepsilon_0(\partial \Phi_e / \partial t)$, where ε_0 is the permittivity of free space and $\partial \Phi e / \partial t$ is the instantaneous rate of change of electric flux. It is not actually a current, but for use in Ampere's law, it is treated like one. Thus, for transient cases, the I in Ampere's law is calculated as $I = I_{actual} + I_d$.

Transformers, generators, and electric motors

Transformers are devices that allow power to be exchanged between two circuits through electromagnetic induction. They generally consist of a pair of coils wrapped around a single metal core. The magnetic field induced by the current in one coil in turn induces a current in the second coil. The amount of current induced in the second coil is dependent on the inducing current and the number of loops in each coil: $I_2/I_1 = N_1/N_2$, where N is the number of loops in the given coil. Since the power given up by the one circuit is the same as that received by the second circuit, we may also say that $V_1 I_1 = V_2 I_2$, or equivalently $I_2/I_1 = V_1/V_2$.

Generators operate by using mechanical energy to turn a coil in a magnetic field, thus converting it to electrical energy. Often, large generators will require gasoline combustion engines to provide the necessary power to operate, though some are able to tap natural power sources such as flowing water. Smaller generators may be powered by hand cranks or stationary bicycles.

Electric motors are basically the reverse of generators. They operate by using an alternating current source connected to an electromagnet to create an oscilating magnetic field that causes a current-carrying coil to rotate, thus generating a torque. DC motors require additional parts to direct the flow of current in such a way that the coil will be continuously rotating.

Faraday's law and Lenz's law

Electromagnetic induction is the process by which current is induced due to a change in magnetic flux. One or more loops of wire in a magnetic field have magnetic flux through them of $\Phi_m =$ $BAcos(\theta)$, where A is the area enclosed by the loop and θ is the angle between a vector normal to the plane of the loop and the magnetic field vector. The produced EMF can be found by Faraday's law, stated in equation form as $V_{emf} = -N(d\Phi_m/dt)$, where N is the number of loops in the coil. So, this induced voltage will exist only as long as Φ_m is changing. A change in any of the variables (B, A,

- 44 -

Copyright © Mometrix Media. You have been licensed one copy of this document for personal use only. Any other reproduction or redistribution is strictly prohibited. All rights reserved.

or θ) can cause a change in magnetic flux. Generators operate by rotating a coil in a constant magnetic field.

The contribution to this concept by Lenz's law is the negative sign in the equation of Faraday's law. Lenz's law states that the induced emf will try to counter the changing magnetic flux by creating a current to produce another magnetic field opposing the change in magnetic flux.

Copyright © Mometrix Media. You have been licensed one copy of this document for personal use only. Any other reproduction or redistribution is strictly prohibited. All rights reserved.

Optics and Waves

Velocity, amplitude, wavelength, and frequency

The velocity of a wave is the rate at which it travels in a given medium. It is defined in the same way that velocity of physical objects is defined, a change in position divided by a change in time. A single wave may have a different velocity for every medium in which it travels. Some types of waves, such as light waves, do not require a medium.

Amplitude is one measure of a wave's strength. It is half the verticle distance between the highest and lowest points on the wave, the crest and trough, respectively. The vertical midpoint, halfway between the crest and trough, is sometimes called an equilibrium point, or a node. Amplitude is often denoted with an A.

The wavelength is the horizontal distance between successive crests or troughs, or the distance between the first and third of three successive nodes. Wavelength is generally denoted as λ.

Frequency is the number of crests or troughs that pass a particular point in a given period of time. It is the inverse of the period, the time required for the wave to cycle from one crest or trough to the next. Frequency, f, is generally measured in hertz, or cycles per second.

Velocity, wavelength, and frequency are not independent quantities. They are related by the expression $v = \lambda f$.

Reflection, transmission, and absorption

When light waves make contact with matter, they are either reflected, transmitted, or absorbed. If the light is reflected from the surface of the matter, the angle at which it hits the surface will be the same as the angle at which it leaves. If the ray of light is perpendicular to the surface, it will be reflected back in the direction from which it came.

When light is transmitted from one medium to another, its direction may be altered upon entering the new medium. This is known as refraction. The degree to which the light is refracted depends on the speed at which light travels in each medium.

Light that is neither reflected nor transmitted will be absorbed by the surface and stored as heat energy. Because there are no ideal surfaces, most light and matter interaction will be a combination of two or even all three of these. Another result of imperfect surfaces is scattering, which occurs when waves are reflected in multiple directions. Rayleigh scattering is the specific case of a light wave being scattered by tiny particles that single out particular wavelengths. Dust particles in the atmosphere scatter primarily the blue wavelength of sunlight to give our sky a predominantly blue hue.

Intensity

Intensity is a physical quantity, equivalent to the flux through a given area over a period of time. It may also be defined as the energy density of a wave times its velocity. Intensity has units of watts

- 46 -

Copyright © Mometrix Media. You have been licensed one copy of this document for personal use only. Any other reproduction or redistribution is strictly prohibited. All rights reserved.

per square meter. The intensity of light decreases as the distance from the light source increases. The inverse square law states that the intensity is inversely proportional to the square of the distance from the source. It is also directly proportional to the power of the light source. This is shown mathematically by the expression $I = CP/r^2$, where C is the proportionality constant. This may be better understood by imagining the light waves emanating from a source as an expanding sphere. As their distance from the source increases as r, the area over which they must divide themselves increases as $4pi*r^2$.

Doppler effect

One common phenomenon of wave motion is the Doppler effect. It is a disparity between the emitted frequency and the observed frequency. It is the caused by relative motion between the wave source and the observer. If the source and observer are both moving toward one another, the observed frequency is determined by the following equation: $f_o = f_e(v_w + v_o)/(v_w - v_s)$, where v_w is the speed of the wave. If the source or the observer is moving in the opposite direction, its sign must be reversed. The Doppler effect is most commonly observed when sound waves change pitch as an observer's relative motion to a train or emergency vehicle changes. The Doppler effect is also employed in the operation of speed-detecting radar guns. Microwaves are emitted at a known frequency and, after being reflected by the object in question, return at a different frequency, giving the object's speed.

Transverse and longitudinal waves

Transverse waves are waves whose oscillations are perpendicular to the direction of motion. A light wave is an example of a transverse wave. A group of light waves traveling in the same direction will be oscillating in several different planes. Light waves are said to be polarized when they are filtered such that only waves oscillating in a particular plane are allowed to pass, with the remainder being absorbed by the filter. If two such polarizing filters are employed successively and aligned to allow different planes of oscillation, they will block all light waves.

Longitudinal waves are waves that oscillate in the same direction as their primary motion. Their motion is restricted to a single axis, so they may not be polarized. A sound wave is an example of a longitudinal wave.

Sound waves

The pitch of a sound as it reaches one's ear is based on the frequency of the sound waves. A high-pitched sound has a higher frequency than a low-pitched sound. Like all waves, sound waves transmit energy. The rate at which this energy is transmitted is the sonic power. Loudness, or intensity of sound, is the sonic power received per unit area.

Beats occur when a pair of sound waves, whose frequencies differ only slightly, interfere with one another. This interference causes a periodic variation in sound intensity, whose frequency is equal to the difference between that of the two sound waves. This is noticeable when tuning two instruments to one another. As the two pitches get closer, the beat frequency will become smaller and smaller until it disappears entirely, indicating that the instruments are in tune.

Copyright © Mometrix Media. You have been licensed one copy of this document for personal use only. Any other reproduction or redistribution is strictly prohibited. All rights reserved.

Resonance and natural frequency

Every physical object has one or more natural frequencies, or frequencies at which it will naturally vibrate. The natural frequency is based on the object's dimensions, density, orientation, and other factors. If the object is acted on by a periodic force, it will vibrate at its natural frequency, regardless of the forcing frequency. If the excitation force is operating at the object's natural frequency, the object will experience resonance, in which the object receives all of the energy exerted by the excitation force. The amplitude of the vibration will increase rapidly and without bound until either the excitation force changes frequency or the natural frequency of the object is altered.

Electromagnetic spectrum

The electromagnetic spectrum is the range of all wavelengths and frequencies of known electromagnetic waves. Visible light occupies only a small portion of the electromagnetic spectrum. Some of the common classifications of electromagnetic waves are listed in the table below with their approximate frequency ranges.

Classification	Freq. (Hz)
Gamma Rays	$\sim 10^{19}$
X-Rays	$\sim 10^{17} - 10^{18}$
Ultraviolet	$\sim 10^{15} - 10^{16}$
Visible Light	$\sim 10^{14}$
Infra-red	$\sim 10^{11} - 10^{14}$
Microwaves	$\sim 10^{10} - 10^{11}$
Radio/TV	$\sim 10^{6} - 10^{9}$

Electromagnetic waves travel at the speed of light, $c = 3 \times 10^8$ m/s. To find the wavelength of any electromagnetic wave, simply divide c by the frequency. Visible light occupies a range of wavelengths from approximately 380 nm (violet) to 740 nm (red). The full spectrum of color can be found between these two wavelengths.

Standing waves

A standing wave is the result of interference between two waves of the same frequency moving in opposite directions. These waves, although in constant motion, have certain points on the wave where the amplitude is zero, locations referred to as nodes. One example of a standing wave is a plucked guitar string. Since the string is attached at both ends, the fixed ends will be nodes. The primary tone will be that of the fundamental, or first harmonic, shown in the first figure below. It has a wavelength of twice the length of the string, L. The other three pictures below are those of the second through fourth harmonics. The nth harmonic has wavelength and frequency of $\lambda_n = 2L/n$ and $f_n = nv/2L$, where v is wave velocity.

Copyright © Mometrix Media. You have been licensed one copy of this document for personal use only. Any other reproduction or redistribution is strictly prohibited. All rights reserved.

This same phenomenon occurs inside the tubes of wind instruments, though it is much more difficult to visualize. With a tube, however, there will be one or two open ends. Rather than a node, each open end will coincide with an antinode: that is, a crest or trough. For waves in a tube with two open ends, the wavelength and frequency calculations are the same as those for the plucked string. For the case with one open end, only the odd harmonics will be seen. The frequency of the nth harmonic becomes $f_n = nv/4L$, where n is odd.

Young's double-slit experiment

Thomas Young's double-slit experiment visually demonstrated the interference between two sets of light waves. It consisted of shining light through two thin, closely spaced parallel slits and onto a screen. The interference between light waves from the two slits caused a pattern of alternately light and dark bands to appear on the screen, due to constructive and destructive interference, respectively. The dimensions of the experimental setup can be used to determine the wavelength of the light being projected onto the screen. This is given by the equation $\lambda = yd/x$, where y is the distance between the centers of two light bands, d is the distance between the slits, and x is the distance from the slits to the screen. Thin-film interference is caused when incident light is reflected both by a partially reflective thin layer on a surface and by the surface itself. This interference may be constructive or destructive.

Wave superposition and interference

The principle of linear superposition states that two or more waves occupying the same space create an effect equal to the sum of their individual amplitudes at that location. This is known as interference. If the resultant amplitude is larger than either individual amplitude, it is constructive interference. Similarly, if the interference reduces the effect, it is considered destructive.

Some special cases of interference are standing waves and beats, in which two waves having the same and nearly the same frequency, respectively, interfere with one another. Another concept related to interference is phase. If two waves with the same frequency are in phase, then they have perfectly constructive interference. The nodes in each wave will line up, as will the respective crests and troughs. If those same two waves are 180 degrees out of phase, they will experience perfectly destructive interference. The nodes will still line up, but each crest will be aligned with a trough, and vice versa. From this it can be seen that constructive interference results in a larger wave amplitude than destructive interference. If two identical waves are 180 degrees out of phase, the resultant wave will have zero amplitude. This effect is the design impetus for some noise-cancellation technology.

Snell's law

When light is transmitted from one medium to another, its direction may be altered upon entering the new medium. This is known as refraction. The degree to which the light is refracted depends on the index of refraction, n, for each medium. The index of refraction is a ratio of the speed of light in a vacuum to the speed of light in the medium in question, $n = c/v_m$. Since light can never travel faster than it does in a vacuum, the index of refraction is always greater than one. Snell's law gives the equation for determining the angle of refraction: $n_1\sin(\theta_1) = n_2\sin(\theta_2)$, where n is the index of refraction for each medium, and θ is the angle the light makes with the normal vector on each side of the interface between the two media.

Copyright © Mometrix Media. You have been licensed one copy of this document for personal use only. Any other reproduction or redistribution is strictly prohibited. All rights reserved.

We will examine a special case by trying to determine the angle of refraction for light traveling from a medium with $n_1 = 3$ to another medium with $n_2 = 1.5$. The light makes an angle $\theta_1 = 35°$ with the normal. Using Snell's law, we find that $\sin(\theta_2) = 1.15$. Since this is not mathematically possible, we conclude that the light cannot be refracted. This case is known as total internal reflection. When light travels from a more dense medium to a less dense medium, there is a minimum angle of incidence, beyond which all light will be reflected. This critical angle is $\theta_1 = \sin^{-1}(n_2/n_1)$. Fiber-optic cables make use of this phenomenon to ensure that the signal is fully reflected internally when it veers into the outer walls of the fiber.

Diffraction and dispersion

Diffraction occurs when a wave encounters a physical object. It includes phenomena such as bending, diverging, and other aperture effects. When light emerges from a single small slit, a rippling effect may be observed. The results of Young's double-slit experiment are due to diffraction as the light waves from these slits diverge. Similarly, light emerging from a circular aperture will project concentric light and dark rings due to diffraction. Diffraction grating is an arrangement of material whose reflective properties are intentionally varied at equally spaced intervals. Due to the arrangement, incident light is reflected in specific directions, known as diffraction orders, based on its wavelength.

Dispersion occurs when light consisting of multiple wavelengths enters a medium whose propagation behavior depends on the wavelength of transmitted light. This is what is observed when light passes through a prism, splitting it into its component colors.

Real and virtual images

In optics, an object's image is what is seen when the object is viewed through a lens. The location of an object's image is related to the lens's focal length by the equation $1/d_o + 1/d_i = 1/f$, where f is the focal length, and d_o and d_i are the distance of the object and its image from the lens, respectively. A positive d_i indicates that the image is on the opposite side of the lens from the object. If the lens is a magnifying lens, the height of the object may be different from that of its image, and may even be inverted. The object's magnification, m, can be found as $m = -d_i/d_o$. The value for the magnification can then be used to relate the object's height to that of its image: $m = y_i/y_o$. Note that if the magnification is negative, then the image has been inverted.

Images may be either real or virtual. Real images are formed by light rays passing through the image location, while virtual images are only perceived by reverse extrapolating refracted light rays. Diverging lenses cannot create real images, only virtual ones. Real images are always on the opposite side of a converging lens from the object and are always inverted.

Thin lenses

A lens is an optical device that redirects light to either converge or diverge in specific geometric patterns. Whether the lens converges or diverges is dependent on the lens being convex or concave, respectively. The particular angle of redirection is dictated by the lens's focal length. For a converging lens, this is the distance from the lens that parallel rays entering from the opposite side would intersect. For a diverging lens, it is the distance from the lens that parallel rays entering the lens would intersect if they were reverse extrapolated. However, the focal length of a diverging lens is always considered to be negative. A thin lens is a lens whose focal length is much greater than its thickness. By making this assumption, we can derive many helpful relations.

Copyright © Mometrix Media. You have been licensed one copy of this document for personal use only. Any other reproduction or redistribution is strictly prohibited. All rights reserved.

Concave mirrors

Concave mirrors will create an image of an object in varying ways depending on the location of the object. The table below details the location, orientation, magnification, and nature of the image. The five object locations to be examined are between the mirror and the focal point (1), at the focal point (2), between the focal point and the center of curvature, or twice the focal point (3), at the center of curvature (4), and beyond the center of curvature (5).

Location	Orient	Magnif	Type
$d_i < 0$	upright	$m > 1$	virtual
none	none	none	none
$d_i > 2f$	inverted	$m < -1$	real
$d_i = 2f$	inverted	$m = -1$	real
$f < d_i < 2f$	inverted	$0 > m > -1$	real

Note in case 5 that the image may effectively be located at the focal point. This is the case for objects at extremely great, or near infinite, distances from the mirror. The magnification at these distances will be very small and a true infinite distance would result in a magnification of zero.

Plane mirrors and spherical mirrors

Plane mirrors have very simple properties. They reflect only virtual images, they have no magnification, and the object's distance from the mirror is always equal to that of its image. Plane mirrors will also appear to reverse the directions left and right.

Spherical mirrors follow the same governing equations for finding image height, location, orientation, and magnification as do thin lenses; however, the sign convention for image location is reversed. A positive image location denotes that it is on the same side as the object. Spherical mirrors may be either concave or convex. Convex mirrors are by far the simpler of the two. They will always reflect virtual, upright images with magnification between zero and one. Concave mirrors have varying behavior based on the object location.

Simple magnifier, the microscope, and the telescope

A simple magnifier, or commonly a magnifying glass, is a converging lens that creates an enlarged virtual image near the observer's eye. The object must be within a certain distance, about 25 cm or 10 inches, from the magnifier for it to operate properly. Otherwise, the image will be blurry.

A microscope is a magnifying device that is used to examine very small objects. It uses a series of lenses to capture light coming from the far side of the sample under examination. Often microscopes will have interchangeable magnification lenses mounted on a wheel, allowing the user to adjust the level of magnification by rotating in a different lens. Optical microscopes will generally be limited to a magnification of 1500.
Telescopes are used to view very distant objects, most often celestial bodies. Telescopes use both lenses and mirrors to capture light from a distant source, focus it, and then magnify it. This creates a virtual image that is very much smaller than the object itself, and yet much larger than the object appears to the naked eye.

Copyright © Mometrix Media. You have been licensed one copy of this document for personal use only. Any other reproduction or redistribution is strictly prohibited. All rights reserved.

Prisms

Prisms are optical devices that alter the path or nature of light waves. Glass and plastic are the two most prevalent materials used to make prisms. There are three different types of prisms in common use. The most familiar of these is the dispersive prism, which splits a beam of light into its constituent wavelengths. For sunlight, this results in the full spectrum of color being displayed. These prisms are generally in the familiar triangular prism shape.
Polarizing prisms, as their name suggests, polarize light, but without significantly reducing the intensity, as a simple filter would. Waves that are oscillating in planes other than the desired plane are caused to rotate, so that they are oscillating in the desired plane. This type of prism is commonly used in cameras.

Reflective prisms are much less common than either of the others. They reflect light, often through the use of the total internal reflection phenomenon. Their primary use is in binoculars.

Copyright © Mometrix Media. You have been licensed one copy of this document for personal use only. Any other reproduction or redistribution is strictly prohibited. All rights reserved.

Scientific Inquiry, Processes, Technology, and Society

Scientific process

Perhaps the most important skill in science is that of observation. A scientist must be able to take accurate data from his experimental setup or from nature without allowing bias to alter the results. Another important skill is hypothesizing. A scientist must be able to combine his knowledge of theory and of other experimental results to logically determine what should occur in his own tests. The data-analysis process requires the twin skills of ordering and categorizing. Gathered data must be arranged in such a way that it is readable and readily shows the key results. A skill that may be integrated with the previous two is comparing. A scientist should be able to compare his own results with other published results. He must also be able to infer, or draw logical conclusions, from his results. He must be able to apply his knowledge of theory and results to create logical experimental designs and determine cases of special behavior. Lastly, a scientist must be able to communicate his results and his conclusions. The greatest scientific progress is made when scientists are able to review and test one another's work and offer advice or suggestions.

Scientific method of inquiry

The scientific method of inquiry is a general method by which ideas are tested and either confirmed or refuted by experimentation. The first step in the scientific method is formulating the problem that is to be addressed. It is essential to clearly define the limits of what is to be observed, since that allows for a more focused analysis. Once the problem has been defined, it is necessary to form a hypothesis. This educated guess should be a possible solution to the problem that was formulated in the first step. The next step is to test that hypothesis by experimentation. This often requires the scientist to design a complete experiment. The key to making the best possible use of an experiment is observation. Observations may be quantitative, that is, when a numeric measurement is taken, or they may be qualitative, that is, when something is evaluated based on feeling or preference. This measurement data will then be examined to find trends or patterns that are present. From these trends, the scientist will then draw conclusions or make generalizations about the results, intended to predict future results. If these conclusions support the original hypothesis, the experiment is complete and the scientist will publish his conclusions to allow others to test them by repeating the experiment. If they do not support the hypothesis, the results should then be used to develop a new hypothesis, which can then be verified by a new or redesigned experiment.

Experimental design

Designing relevant experiments that allow for meaningful results is not a simple task. Every stage of the experiment must be carefully planned to ensure that the right data can be safely and accurately taken. Ideally, an experiment should be controlled so that all of the conditions except the ones being manipulated are held constant. This helps to ensure that the results are not skewed by unintended consequences of shifting conditions. A good example of this is a placebo group in a drug trial. All other conditions are the same, but that group is not given the medication. In addition to proper control, it is important that the experiment be designed with data collection in mind. For instance, if the quantity to be measured is temperature, there must be a temperature device such as a thermocouple integrated into the experimental setup. While the data are being collected, they

Copyright © Mometrix Media. You have been licensed one copy of this document for personal use only. Any other reproduction or redistribution is strictly prohibited. All rights reserved.

should periodically be checked for obvious errors. If there are data points that are orders of magnitude from the expected value, then it might be a good idea to make sure that no experimental errors are being made, either in data collection or condition control. Once all the data have been gathered, they must be analyzed. The way in which this should be done depends on the type of data and the type of trends observed. It may be useful to fit curves to the data to determine if the trends follow a common mathematical form. It may also be necessary to perform a statistical analysis of the results to determine what effects are significant. Finally, the data should be presented in a clear and logical fashion.

Scientific statements

Hypotheses are educated guesses about what is likely to occur, and are made to provide a starting point from which to begin design of the experiment. They may be based on results of previously observed experiments or knowledge of theory, and follow logically forth from these. Assumptions are statements that are taken to be fact without proof for the purpose of performing a given experiment. They may be entirely true, or they may be true only for a given set of conditions under which the experiment will be conducted. Assumptions are necessary to simplify experiments; indeed, many experiments would be impossible without them. Models are mathematical relationships that attempt to represent the reality of a much more complicated natural system. They do this by simplifying or ignoring certain factors that would be impossible to accurately represent in a simple mathematical relationship. Models are useful tools for testing ideas that would be difficult to test in a physical system, but they cannot reflect the totality of what is occurring or would occur. Laws are statements that describe natural behavior, which have been shown to hold true through repeated testing. A law is often stated as a mathematical relationship. Like everything else in science, laws are not immune to challenge. If repeatable testing demonstrates that a law does not hold true, the law must be modified or discarded. A theory is a statement that seeks to explain why a particular phenomenon occurs. Unlike a law, it focuses on the process by which observed behavior takes place, as opposed to simply describing what takes place.

Overarching concepts

There are several concepts that transcend the various branches of science and can be found as integral parts of physics, chemistry, biology, and other areas of study. One of these concepts is the system. A system is an arbitrarily sized group of entities that are taken to be a single unit. Systems may consist of physical bodies or of abstract concepts that intertwine. Systems will often be modeled by either mathematical expressions or physical-scale models, depending on the type of system and the purpose of the scale. In scale models, it is important to keep in mind that scale can have a huge effect on the behavior of a system. This can be clearly seen in models of the solar system. The gravitational effects in a room-sized solar system model will be entirely negligible due to its reduced size. Other phenomena, such as nuclear attractive forces, will only be observed on the atomic level. If the state of a system is constant, it is at equilibrium. Equilibrium may be either static or dynamic. For example, a pair of side-by-side pools are in static equilibrium if there is no water being transferred between them. They are in dynamic equilibrium if equal amounts of water are being transferred between the pools in each direction. In the design of physical components, something that may be encountered is the interrelationship between form and function. If one of these two goals takes priority, that one will dictate the other. For instance, if the external appearance of a building is considered to be of higher importance than its utility, the functionality of the building may be limited.

Copyright © Mometrix Media. You have been licensed one copy of this document for personal use only. Any other reproduction or redistribution is strictly prohibited. All rights reserved.

Scientific measurement and unit systems

The basis of quantitative measurement is the unit system. In order to properly describe how large, how heavy, or how hot something is, it is necessary to have some reference unit. The most commonly used unit system in the world is the SI, short for the Systeme International d'Unites, although the English system is still in popular use in the United States. In SI, there are base units and derived units. Derived units may be stated as some combination of the base units. The SI base units for length, mass, time, temperature, and electric current are meter (m), kilogram (kg), second (s), kelvin (K), and ampere (A), respectively. Some common derived units are newtons ($kg\text{-}m/s^2$) and pascals ($kg/m\text{-}s^2$). Most SI units can be scaled up or down by adding a prefix. To alter a unit by 10^3, 10^6, or 10^9, add a prefix of kilo (k), mega (M), or giga (G). For instance, a kilometer (km) is 10^3 meters. To change the unit by a factor of 10^{-3}, 10^{-6}, or 10^{-9}, add a prefix of milli (m), micro (μ), or nano (n). For instance, a microsecond (μs) is 10^{-6} seconds. It is important to note that the SI base unit kilogram has already employed a prefix to scale up the smaller unit, gram (g). Order of magnitude is a concept that deals with comparison between two values. If one value differs from the other by a factor of 10^n, it may be said that it differs by n orders of magnitude.

Other SI base units include the mole and the candela. Some lesser used prefixes include: hecto (h), 10^2; deca (da), 10^1; deci (d), 10^{-1}; and centi (c), 10^{-2}.

Scientific knowledge

Perhaps the greatest peculiarity of scientific knowledge is that, at the same time that it is taken as fact, it may be disproved. Current scientific knowledge is the basis from which new discoveries are made. Yet even knowledge that has stood for hundreds of years is not considered too infallible to be challenged. If someone can create an experiment whose results consistently and reproducibly defy a law that has been in place for generations, that law will be nullified. It is absolutely essential, however, that these reproductions of the experiment be conducted by many different scientists who are in isolation from one another so there is no bias or interacting effects on the results.

Interpretation of tables, charts, and graphs

One of the reasons data are so often plotted on graphs is that this format makes it much easier to see trends and draw conclusions. For instance, on a simple position vs. time graph, the slope of the curve indicates the object's velocity at each point in time. If the curve becomes level, this means the object is not moving. In a simple velocity vs. time graph, the slope of the curve indicates the object's acceleration at each point in time. Additionally, the area contained under the curve indicates the total distance traveled. For instance, if the object is traveling at a constant 5 m/s for 10 s, the velocity vs. time graph will be a straight line at $y = 5$ between $x = 0$ and $x = 10$. The area under this curve is $(5\ m/s)(10\ s) = 50\ m$. Thus, the object traveled 50 meters.

Nearly any type of quantity may be graphed, so it is important to always check the axis labels to ensure that you know what the graph represents and what units are being used.

Data collection and analysis

In order to take data measurements from their experimental setups, scientists will often use measurement devices wired to a computer running data-acquisition software. This allows them to take numerous readings per second if necessary. Once the data is collected, it will often be

Copyright © Mometrix Media. You have been licensed one copy of this document for personal use only. Any other reproduction or redistribution is strictly prohibited. All rights reserved.

organized using a spreadsheet, such as Microsoft Excel. This multipurpose program contains several options for displaying the data in graphs or charts, as well as tools for performing statistical analyses or linear regressions. Linear regression is a technique used to determine whether gathered data fits a particular trend or equation. It attempts to fit a common line or curve equation to the data set. A very important concept to understand when taking data is that of significant figures. Significant figures, or significant digits, indicate how precisely a quantity is known. Each non-zero digit is always significant. A zero is significant if either: 1) it is to the right of both a non-zero digit and the decimal point; or 2) it is between two other significant digits. For instance, 1.0230 has five significant figures while 0.0230 has only three because the trailing zero is the only zero to the right of both a non-zero and the decimal. When multiplying (or dividing), the product (quotient) has as many significant figures as the factor (dividend or divisor) with the fewest. When adding (or subtracting), the sum (difference) should be rounded to the highest final decimal place of the involved terms.

(3.4 + 56.78 = 60.18 --> 60.2, three significant figures)

Data errors and error analysis

No measurements are ever 100% accurate. There is always some amount of error regardless of how careful the observer or how good his equipment. The important thing for the scientist to know is how much error is present in a given measurement. Two commonly misunderstood terms regarding error are accuracy and precision. Accuracy is a measure of how close a measurement is to the true value. Precision is a measure of how close repeated measurements are to one another. Error is usually quantified using a confidence interval and an uncertainty value. For instance, if the quantity is measured as 100 ± 2 on a 95% confidence interval, this means that there is a 95% chance that the actual value falls between 98 and 102.

When looking for the uncertainty in a derived quantity such as density, the errors in the constituent quantities, mass and volume in this case, are propagated to the derived quantity. The percent uncertainty in the density, U_ρ/ρ, can be found by the equation:
$U_\rho/\rho = sqrt((U_m/m)^2 + (U_V/V)^2)$.

Basic safety procedures

The most important safety precaution is to be prepared. Be acquainted with all potential hazards of any procedure, as well as all equipment, its associated safety procedures, and all lab manuals before beginning an experiment. Calibrate all equipment properly and handle it with care and only for its intended purpose. Read all safety data sheets before beginning a procedure. Perform all procedures yourself before assigning them to students.

Secure and label all biological, chemical, and carcinogenic materials, away from heat and food, not on a high surface or on the floor, and segregated by reactivity. Follow all local disposal procedures for used lab materials, labeling all chemical and biological waste. Make sure all storage and waste containers are leakproof.

Avoid contamination. Use distilled water in the lab, not tap water, as tap water contains impurities. Clean and rinse all glassware after use.

Secure items with clamps as necessary. Use, and have students use, goggles, gloves, and lab coats. Take extra caution with knives, glass rods, weights, and any potentially injurious materials.

Copyright © Mometrix Media. You have been licensed one copy of this document for personal use only. Any other reproduction or redistribution is strictly prohibited. All rights reserved.

Heat

Periodically check the gas connections and burners in the laboratory. Unless the gas is actively being used, keep the master gas valve off at all times. Never heat anything in a closed container, where pressure can build, and use only glassware approved for lab use. Use gloves, goggles, and fire-retardant pads as needed around hot materials. Never place a heat source in a location where it can be knocked over accidentally. Keep all flames and gas water heaters far from the vapors of flammable liquids.

Pressure

When using a pressure cooker, never exceed 20 pounds per square inch of pressure. Never open a hot pressure cooker. Always make sure the safety valve is in working order.

Electrical

Know the location of the main cutoff switch for the laboratory. Regularly check all electrical connections, live wires, and batteries before turning the power on. All outlets should be GFCI, and extension cords should only be used extremely judiciously.

Keep all electrical current away from flammable materials and water. Use only 6 or 12-volt direct current, and double-insulate or ground all power equipment.

In all procedures, the insertion of the plug should be the last step in setup; when disassembling, remove the plug first. Use only one hand in all procedures involving an electrical current. Never allow oneself or a student to become part of an electrical circuit.

Sound

Never exceed 110 decibels, which causes hearing damage. When using a high-speed siren disk, make sure to use the safety disk.

Radiation

Shield all people properly when using X-rays, and keep them at least 10 feet from any radiation experiment. Periodically check all tubes, including vacuum, heat effect, magnetic, and deflection tubes. Enclose cathode rays in a frame, never allow students to use them themselves, and operate them for the shortest possible time and at the lowest practical voltage.

Radioactivity

Ensure you have access to a radiation survey meter before doing any radioactivity experiment, and make sure you have been trained properly in equipment handling, demonstration, and disposal procedures. Never use bare hands to handle radioactive materials. Shield all people from all radioactive material as required, by paper, glass, or lead. Store all radioactive material securely, and dispose of it properly.

Light

Do not use broken mirrors, prisms, or glass; grind or tape those with sharp edges. Periodically check all connections for spectroscopic light voltage. Shield all people from ultraviolet and infrared light sources. Be aware of students with neurological conditions (for instance, epilepsy) that make them susceptible to strobe lights. Never allow students to look directly into the sun; design viewfinders for solar-eclipse viewing.

Copyright © Momatrix Media. You have been licensed one copy of this document for personal use only. Any other reproduction or redistribution is strictly prohibited. All rights reserved.

Lasers

Be aware of the laser classification system, and know which type you are using. Shield all people from direct exposure to a laser; contain people's movements when using lasers to avoid inadvertent exposure. Project lasers only onto non-reflective surfaces, maintain a sufficient light level to prevent pupil dilation, and make sure to shield all prisms and reflective objects. Use the minimum effective optical power. Terminate the beam at a point beyond the furthest point of interest, in a non-reflective material. Be familiar with the safety features of a laser projector, and use beam stops when the laser is not actively being used. Equip the laser with a key switch if possible.

Basic safety rules

It is critical to plan for all eventualities when it comes to laboratory safety. Maintain all safety equipment and know how to use it. Understand first-aid procedures and re-familiarize yourself with the relevant ones when planning student experiments.

Distribute safety rules to students, and keep instructions for all safety procedures readily available for all parties. Post multiple and clear signs warning of any dangers associated with hazardous chemicals or delicate equipment. Post copies of all laboratory rules and spell out appropriate material-handling procedures.

Be prepared and willing to seek help in the event of an emergency. Students should never clean chemical or biological spills; only the teacher should, using appropriate chemical spill kits or bleach as appropriate. Large spills must be reported to the school administration and the fire department as soon as possible. You must also immediately report any injuries or accidents to the school administration and a health provider.

Students must wear safety goggles during heating, dissecting, and using acids and bases. Long hair should be tied back, and hands washed before and after experiments. Food must be forbidden in the lab.

Setting up a science laboratory

The most important safety guideline in setting up a laboratory is to plan well and become familiar with all equipment and materials. Understand theoretically as well as practically the risks and effects of all materials you are using; know how to neutralize the effects of all materials. Set up all equipment so that it is in no danger of falling. Verify the locations and functionality of all safety equipment. Regularly monitor the condition and stock of all materials, including safety materials. Always choose the least hazardous effective materials for all procedures.

Perform all experiments yourself before doing them with students. Provide clear instructions on all procedures, including waste-disposal procedures, to students before having them perform them. Reinforce students' knowledge of safety procedures throughout the term.
Keep the laboratory locked at all times when not in use.

Legal Responsibilities

At all levels of the legal system, it is the responsibility of a teacher to provide a safe environment for students. Never leave the room accessible to unsupervised students; if you must leave the room, provide students with proper alternative supervision. Familiarize students with safety procedures,

Copyright © Mometrix Media. You have been licensed one copy of this document for personal use only. Any other reproduction or redistribution is strictly prohibited. All rights reserved.

and review them regularly. Posting the rules is insufficient; you must continually review them with students. If a procedure cannot be safely carried out, it must not be performed.

Avoid negligence. Always consider all possible outcomes before performing a procedure, and exercise care to minimize any danger to students and property. State Departments of Education have encoded the specific legal responsibilities of science teachers; familiarize yourself with state laws.

Basic safety equipment

All labs should contain the following items:
- Bucket of sand for absorption of spills and smothering of alkali fires
- Fire blanket
- First-aid kit, containing bandages and antiseptic
- One GFCI within two feet of all water supplies
- Exit signs
- Emergency shower
- Emergency eyewash station
- Splashproof eye protection for all parties, and a means to sanitize it
- Face shields
- Emergency exhaust fans that vent to the outside of the building
- Fire blanket
- Gloves, both rubber and nitrile
- Master cutoff switches for gas, electricity, and compressed air
- ABC fire extinguisher
- Storage cabinets for flammable items
- Chemical spill-control kit
- Fume hood with a spark-proof motor
- Flame-retardant lab aprons
- Mercury clean-up kit
- Neutralizing agents, including acetic acid and sodium bicarbonate
- Signs drawing attention to potential hazards
- Segregated, clearly labeled containers for storing broken glassware, flammable items, solid chemicals, corrosive items, and waste.

Major energy issues

Since the Industrial Revolution, energy for industrialized human needs has come from fossil fuels, particularly coal and petroleum, but increased use means that this source of fuel is quickly being depleted, in addition to causing pollution. The search for alternative, safe sources of energy for an increasingly industrialized world population is therefore increasingly important to scientists.

An ideal source of energy would be efficient, renewable, and sustainable. Various sources of alternative energy have been proposed, including wind, water, solar, nuclear, geothermal, and biomass, but thus far none have been made practically available on a large scale. Some, such as wind and water, blight the landscape, while the conversion methods for other sources, such as solar and biomass, are still relatively inefficient. The scientific community is still unclear on the best way to harness the power of photosynthesis and biomass for energy needs in a way that would allow a

Copyright © Mometrix Media. You have been licensed one copy of this document for personal use only. Any other reproduction or redistribution is strictly prohibited. All rights reserved.

large-scale energy industry to use it. Scientists remain at work studying the long-term solutions to an increasingly urgent problem for humanity.

Effects of improvements in scientific and technological knowledge

Since the Industrial Revolution, technological improvements to agricultural production have made agriculture productive on an industrial scale, while advances in medical knowledge have brought about the cures for many diseases. People in many parts of the world live longer and enjoy a higher standard of living than ever before.

However, this progress does not come without a price. The effects on the environment of industrialization are almost exclusively negative. Monoculture farming practices resulting from industrialization mean that farming no longer exists as a closed ecosystem; the chemical fertilizers that create record crop yields have changed the nutrient environment, and the waste products of industrial agriculture pollute the water rather than fertilizing the soil. Increased travel creates dangerous carbon dioxide emissions and depletes the earth's limited store of fossil fuels. Water pollution means limited access to potable water, and deforestation has begun to change the makeup of ecosystems and cause the extinction of many species. Through the increased contact made available by improved technology, however, humans are also collaborating on solutions to these new problems.

Increased production of consumer goods

Electric-based, industrial production of manufactured goods has led to an increase in the standard of living for many, especially those in the industrialized world. Consumer goods are produced more cheaply than ever before, since the means of production is not as dependent on the physical abilities of human beings. Scientific advancements have led to a huge number of new synthetic materials from which goods can be made, including plastics and nylon.

However, this increased production damages the environment. Waste products are now created of which humans can make no use, a new phenomenon. Trash created from these new products is buried in landfills, where it has no access to the air, water, and sunlight that are a necessary part of biodegradation; trash made from some synthetic materials does not biodegrade at all. While some waste products can be recycled, many byproducts of industrial manufacturing are hazardous, with no safe way to dispose of them. The long-term sustainability of the environment as a result of massively increased consumer production is an issue of increasing urgency for scientists.

Nuclear power controversy

Nuclear fission power, while sustainable, has a host of attendant controversial problems. Among them is the incredibly dangerous transportation and long-term storage of its radioactive waste products, for which there is still no safe long-term solution. Its effects on those environments and creatures that come in contact with nuclear waste are still largely unknown. In addition, nuclear materials can be used in weaponry, and accidents at nuclear power plants like the one at Chernobyl can be devastating for thousands of years.

Scientists continue their study of the process of nuclear fusion, hoping that if humans can learn to harness the energy produced by smashing atoms rather than splitting them, the attendant problems of nuclear waste storage will be minimized.

Copyright © Mometrix Media. You have been licensed one copy of this document for personal use only. Any other reproduction or redistribution is strictly prohibited. All rights reserved.

Management of non-renewable resources

Non-renewable resources include minerals, which are created naturally over millions of years. The industrialized world extracts minerals for fuel as well as for use in electronic equipment and medicine. Increased human extraction of non-renewable resources has endangered their availability, and over-mining has created other ecological problems, including runoff and water pollution. The use of fossil fuels for energy and transportation causes air pollution and is unsustainable. Fossil fuels cannot be replaced once depleted, and they are being depleted at an increasing rate. The need to find a sustainable alternative to the use of non-renewable fossil fuels is imperative.

Management of renewable resources

Natural resources can be divided into two types, renewable and non-renewable. Renewable resources include plants and animals, along with water, air, and soil.

A pre-industrial earth was a self-sustaining system, maintaining a natural balance among plants, animals, and non-living elements in which waste products from one natural process were the fuel for another. Modern humans have intervened in this process in a way that upsets the natural balance of life. Humans have introduced non-native species from one part of the world to another, resulting in the devastation of local populations. Industrial-scale buildings can create disasters for local ecosystems, ruining habitats for animal populations.

Humans remove an increasing amount of the world's resources for industrial use, too quickly for nature to recover from easily. Renewable resources must be carefully managed to maintain a balanced ecosystem; over-harvesting of forests or over-hunting of animal populations can be devastating. Pollution of the air and water with chemical pollutants has far-reaching effects on the ecosystems of the earth, including the depletion of the ozone layer that protects earth life from ultraviolet rays, as does the removal of forests that produce the earth's oxygen.

Social impacts of science and technology

Recent developments in science and technology have had both positive and negative effects on human society. The issue of sustainable growth is an increasingly important one, as humans realize that the resources they use are not unlimited. Genetic research into diseases, stem cell research, and cloning technology have created great controversies as they have been introduced, and an increasing number of people reject the morality of scientific practices like animal testing in the pursuit of scientific advancement. In addition, an increasingly technology-based world has produced a new social inequality based on access to computers and Internet technology.

These issues are beginning to be debated at all levels of human government, from city councils to the United Nations. Does science provide the authoritative answer to all human problems, or do ethics carry weight in scientific debates as well? Ultimately, humans must weigh the competing needs of facilitating scientific pursuits and maintaining an ethical society as they face new technological questions.

Copyright © Mometrix Media. You have been licensed one copy of this document for personal use only. Any other reproduction or redistribution is strictly prohibited. All rights reserved.

Recent applications of science and technology

Scientific and technological developments have led to the widespread availability of technologies heretofore unheard of, including cellular phones, satellite-based applications, and a worldwide network of connected computers. Some of the notable recent applications include:

Health care: Antibiotics, genetic screening for diseases, the sequencing of the human genome. Issues include problems with health care distribution on an increasingly industrialized planet.

The environment: Computerized models of climate change and pollution monitoring. Issues include increased pollution of the water, air, and soil, and the over-harvesting of natural resources with mechanized equipment.

Agriculture: Genetic improvements in agricultural practices, including increased output on the same amount of arable land. Issues include unknown environmental effects of hybrid species, cross-pollination with organic species, and pollution caused by synthetic chemical fertilizers. Information technology: New Internet-based industries, increased worldwide collaboration, and access to information. Issues include the depletion of natural resources for electronics production.

Contributing individuals to physics

Archimedes (ancient Greece)

Archimedes designed the compound pulley, articulated the principles of the lever, and made important contributions to engineering and geometry, calculating the area of a sphere and an ellipse and approximating the value of pi. Archimedes' Law of the Lever states that when objects are set at distances reciprocally proportional to their respective weights, they are in equilibrium.

Amedeo Avogadro (Italian, 18th century)

Avogadro established the principles of molarity, clarified the relationship between atoms and molecules, and formalized what became known as Avogadro's principle: that equal volumes of gases held at the same pressure and temperature will contain an equal number of molecules, and that their masses will be proportionate to their respective molecular weights. Avogadro's constant is the number of particles present in 1 mole of any substance.

Robert Boyle (Irish, 17th century)

Though regarded as the first modern chemist, Boyle also distinguished himself in physics and contributed to experimental design. Boyle's Law is a mathematical expression of the relationship between volume and pressure within an ideal gas.

Sir Isaac Newton (English, 17th/18th century)

Newton, one of the most important scientists of all time, made critical breakthroughs in the understanding of scientific methods, motion, and optics. Newton described universal gravitation, observed that white light contains the entire spectrum of colors, and discovered the calculus independently of Leibniz (who is credited with it). The three Newtonian laws of motion are:
- An object in motion (or at rest) remains in motion (or at rest) unless acted upon by an external force.
- Force equals mass times acceleration.
- For every action, there is an equal and opposite reaction.

Copyright © Mometrix Media. You have been licensed one copy of this document for personal use only. Any other reproduction or redistribution is strictly prohibited. All rights reserved.

Galileo Galilei (Italian, 17th century)
Galileo determined that all bodies, regardless of mass, fall at the same rate. He argued that motion is continuous, changed only when an external force is applied to it (later incorporated in Newton's laws of motion). His work in astronomy was important in confirming Copernicus' heliocentric model of the solar system. His principle of relativity states that the laws of physics are constant within a constantly moving system, a theory that became central to Einstein's work on relativity.

Marie Curie (Polish/French, 19th century)
Curie was the foremost pioneer of radioactivity. She isolated the radioactive elements polonium and radium, and established that radioactivity was a property of an atom itself rather than of the relationship between multiple molecules.

Michael Faraday (English, 18th/19th century)
Faraday's most important work was in the fields of electromagnetism and electrochemistry. His work led directly to some of the most important breakthroughs in electrical technology of the twentieth century. Faraday introduced the concept of fields to the study of magnetism and electricity. He discovered what would become known as the Faraday Effect, the effect of a strong magnetic field on the behavior of light rays. The Farad (the SI unit of capacitance) and the Faraday constant (the amount of charge on one mole of electrons) are both named for him.

Wilhelm Ostwald (Latvian, 19th/20th century)
One of the founders of classical physical chemistry, Ostwald did important work on the properties of atomic particles, and defined a mole as the molecular weight, in grams, of a given substance.

Albert Einstein (German, 20th century)
Einstein, the most famous twentieth-century scientist, was a theoretical physicist whose special theory of relativity describes the relationship of time and space, and mass and gravity. In it, he declared that gravity is a consequence of the properties of space-time and that the speed of light is constant. He hypothesized that electromagnetic energy can be absorbed or expelled by matter in quanta, and discovered the photoelectric effect.

Stephen Hawking (English, 20th/21st century)
Hawking's principal fields of research are theoretical cosmology and quantum gravity. Expanding on Einstein's work, he has hypothesized about the physical properties of black holes, described conditions necessary for a singularity, and made important contributions in string theory, in an attempt to generalize Einstein's special theory of relativity.

J. Robert Oppenheimer (American, 20th century)
Oppenheimer's scientific contributions are in astrophysics, nuclear physics, and quantum field theory. He served as scientific director of the Manhattan Project, which constructed the first atomic bomb.

Linus Pauling (American, 20th century)
Pauling applied new discoveries in quantum mechanics to the field of chemistry, pioneering the study of molecular medicine. He researched the biochemical origins of genetic diseases like sickle-cell anemia.

Copyright © Mometrix Media. You have been licensed one copy of this document for personal use only. Any other reproduction or redistribution is strictly prohibited. All rights reserved.

Enrico Fermi (Italian/American, 20th century)
Fermi discovered the process of making elements artificially radioactive by bombarding them with neutrons. He divided elements into the two groups of fermions and bosons. His work on nuclear reactions led him to participate in the Manhattan Project.

Niels Bohr (Danish, 20th century)
Bohr established that the number of electrons determined the atom's chemical properties. He articulated the organization of electrons, in discrete orbits around an atom's nucleus, and that electrons could move orbits, thereby emitting radiation—the basis for quantum theory. Bohr worked on the Manhattan Project along with Oppenheimer and Fermi.

Copyright © Mometrix Media. You have been licensed one copy of this document for personal use only. Any other reproduction or redistribution is strictly prohibited. All rights reserved.

Practice Test

Practice Questions

1. Which of the following measurements has the most significant digits?
    a. 0.2990
    b. 2.9900
    c. 2.997
    d. 0.00209

2. The masses of four different objects taken with different scales were 23.04 g, 7.12 g, 0.0088 g and 5.423 g. What is the total mass of all four objects to the proper number of significant digits?
    a. 35.59180 g
    b. 35.5918 g
    c. 35.60 g
    d. 35.59 g

3. Which of the following is a vector quantity?
    a. Distance
    b. Speed
    c. Velocity
    d. Time

4. A person walks 4 meters in a single direction. He or she then changes directions and walks an additional 9 meters. What is the total magnitude of the displacement of the person?
    a. It is 13 meters.
    b. It is always larger than 9 meters but less than 13 meters.
    c. It is less than 13 meters and as small as 5 meters.
    d. It is less than 5 meters.

5. Consider the two vectors below:
Vector A:

Vector B:

Which vector best represents the vector obtained by subtracting A from B ($\vec{B} - \vec{A}$)?

    a.

    c.

    b.

    d.

- 65 -

Copyright © Mometrix Media. You have been licensed one copy of this document for personal use only. Any other reproduction or redistribution is strictly prohibited. All rights reserved.

6. A perfectly circular track has a circumference of 400 meters. A runner goes around the track in 100 seconds instead of her usual time of 80 seconds because a leg cramp causes her to stop running for 20 seconds. What is her average speed?
   a. 0 m/s
   b. 5 m/s
   c. 4 m/s
   d. 20 m/s

7. An automobile increased its speed uniformly from 20 m/s to 30 m/s at rate 5 m/s². During this time it traveled 50 meters. How long did it take the automobile to make this change?
   a. 5 seconds
   b. 2 seconds
   c. 10 seconds
   d. Can't be determined.

8. You throw a baseball straight up near the surface of Earth and it falls back to the ground. Which statement is true about the acceleration of the baseball at the top of its path? [Ignore air resistance]
   a. The acceleration is zero.
   b. The acceleration changes sign.
   c. The acceleration is -9.8 m/s².
   d. The acceleration continues to increase.

9. A space station is revolving in a circular orbit around Earth. Consider the following three statements:
I. The center of mass of the space station is necessarily located at its geometric center.
II. The center of mass is moving at a constant velocity.
III. The center of mass of the space station is moving at a constant speed.
Which of the following statements is true?
   a. I is true.
   b. II is true.
   c. III is true.
   d. I, II, and III are not true.

10. Which of the following demonstrations best illustrates Newton's first law?
   a. Giving a billiard ball at rest on a smooth level table a small push and letting it roll on the table.
   b. Dragging a box on a table at a constant speed by exerting a force just enough to overcome the force of friction.
   c. Trying without success to move a heavy bureau or filing cabinet on the floor.
   d. Running a current through two parallel wires.

11. Consider the following statements about Newton's law:
I. A newton is a fundamental unit.
II. Mass and acceleration are inversely related when the force is constant.
III. Newton's first law can be derived from Newton's second law.
IV. Newton's second law can be derived from the universal law of gravity.
Which of the following statements are true?
   a. I, II, and III.
   b. II and III only.
   c. III only.
   d. I, II, III, and IV are not true.

- 66 -

Copyright © Mometrix Media. You have been licensed one copy of this document for personal use only. Any other reproduction or redistribution is strictly prohibited. All rights reserved.

12. A box with a weight of 10 newtons is resting on a table. Which statement is true?
   a. The force of the table on the box is the reaction to the weight of the box.
   b. The force of the box on the table is the reaction to the weight of the box.
   c. A 10 newton force on Earth is the reaction force.
   d. There is no reaction force because the system is in equilibrium.

13. A lead sphere 10 centimeters in diameter is attached to a 10-meter wire and suspended from a beam in a large warehouse. A lead sphere 1 meter in diameter is hung next to the smaller sphere, almost touching. Ignoring friction, which statement is true?
   a. The small sphere will move slightly towards the big sphere, but the big sphere will not move.
   b. The big sphere will move slightly toward the small sphere, but the small sphere will not move.
   c. Neither sphere will move.
   d. Both spheres will move slightly towards each other.

14. In an amusement park ride, you stand on the floor of a cylindrical ring with your back touching the wall. The ring begins to rotate, slowly at first, but then faster and faster. When the ring is rotating fast enough, the floor is removed. You do not slide down but remained pressed against the wall of the ring. Which is the best explanation for why you don't fall down?
   a. The centripetal force pushes you towards the wall.
   b. The centripetal force changes the direction of your motion.
   c. The force of friction between the wall and your body is greater than your weight.
   d. The rotating ring creates a weightless environment.

15. Bobsled tracks are flat when they are going straight, but when there is a turn, the track is angled (banked) to create a centripetal force. Assuming no friction, the banking angle is θ, the radius of curvature is r, and the maximum speed the bobsled can have without moving off the track is v. If the radius of curvature is doubled and the banking angle remains the same, which of the following statements is true?
   a. The maximum speed is $2v$.
   b. The maximum speed is $4v$.
   c. The maximum speed is $1.4v$.
   d. The maximum speed depends on the banking angle.

Copyright © Mometrix Media. You have been licensed one copy of this document for personal use only. Any other reproduction or redistribution is strictly prohibited. All rights reserved.

16. Two spring scales having negligible mass are connected together and used to weigh a 10 kg object, as shown below.

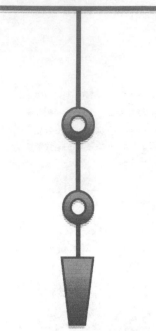

What will be the reading on the scales?
    a. Both scales will read 10 pounds.
    b. Each scale will read 49 newtons.
    c. The sum of the two readings will be 196 newtons.
    d. The bottom scale will read 98 newtons and the top scale will read 0 newtons.

17. A 10-kg plastic block is at rest on a flat wooden surface. The coefficient of static friction between wood and plastic is 0.6 and the coefficient of kinetic friction is 0.5. How much horizontal force is needed to start the plastic box moving?
    a. 5 N
    b. 49 N
    c. 59 N
    d. 98

Copyright © Mometrix Media. You have been licensed one copy of this document for personal use only. Any other reproduction or redistribution is strictly prohibited. All rights reserved.

18. The diagram below shows a force F pulling a box up a ramp against the force of friction and the force of gravity. Which of the following diagrams correctly includes vectors representing the normal force, the force of gravity and the force of friction?

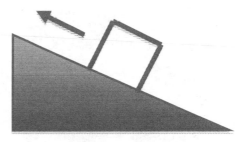

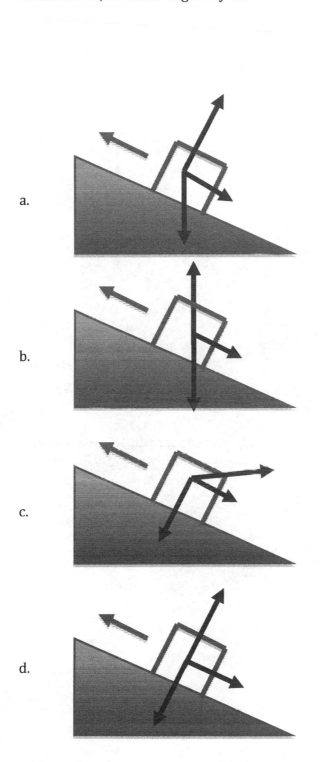

a.

b.

c.

d.

Copyright © Mometrix Media. You have been licensed one copy of this document for personal use only. Any other reproduction or redistribution is strictly prohibited. All rights reserved.

19. The ideal mechanical advantage (IMA) of a pulley system indicates how much force is required to lift a mass. A fixed puley has an IMA of 1 because all it only changes the direction of the force. A floating pulley has an IMA of 2. The total IMA is the product of the individual pulleys' IMAs. What is the ideal mechanical advantage of the pulley system below?

a. 1
b. 2
c. 3
d. 4

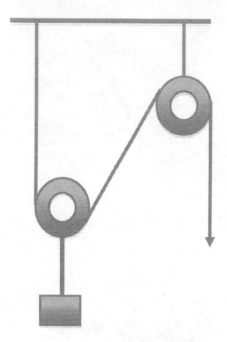

20. The pulley in the device below has no mass and is frictionless. The larger mass is 30 kg and the smaller mass is 20 kg. What is the acceleration of the masses?

a. 0.5 m/s²
b. 2 m/s²
c. 9.8 m/s²
d. 98 m/s²

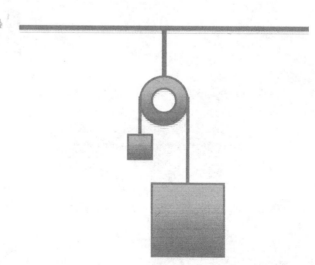

Copyright © Mometrix Media. You have been licensed one copy of this document for personal use only. Any other reproduction or redistribution is strictly prohibited. All rights reserved.

21. A force of 25.0 N pulls three blocks connected by a string on a frictionless surface. What is the tension in the rope between the 4.0-kg block and the 2.0-kg block?

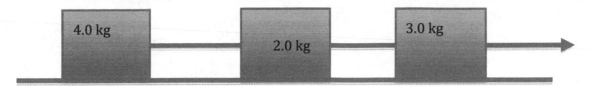

   a. 0 N
   b. 11.1 N
   c. 16.7 N
   d. 25 N

22. A piece of art of mass 200 kg is suspended from two nails so that the angle the hanging wires make is 40° with the horizontal. What is the tension in the hanging wires? (Note: Sin 40° = 0.64 and Cos 40° = 0.77).
   a. 1279 N
   b. 1524 N
   c. 1960 N
   d. 3048 N

23. Two unequal masses are balanced on a fulcrum using a massless bar, as shown below. If both masses are shifted towards the fulcrum so that their distances from the fulcrum are one-half the original distance, what happens to the masses?

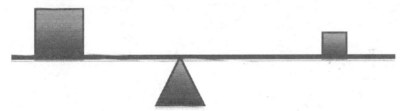

   a. The heavier mass will tilt downward.
   b. The masses will remain balanced.
   c. Cannot be determined from the information given.
   d. The lighter mass will tilt downward.

Copyright © Mometrix Media. You have been licensed one copy of this document for personal use only. Any other reproduction or redistribution is strictly prohibited. All rights reserved.

24. Which of the forces depicted below produces a counter-clockwise torque around the pivot point?

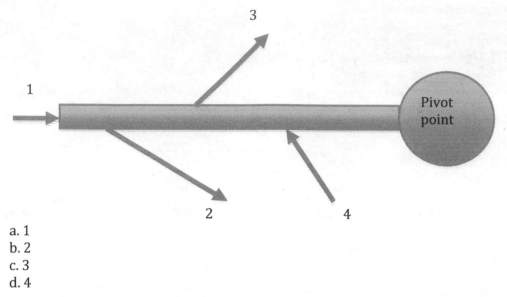

a. 1
b. 2
c. 3
d. 4

25. You blow up a rubber balloon and hold the opening tight with your fingers. You then release your fingers, causing air to blow out of the balloon. This pushes the balloon forward, causing the balloon to shoot across the room. Which of Newton's laws best explains the cause of this motion?
a. First law
b. Second law
c. Third law
d. Law of gravity

26. Which has a greater moment of inertia about an axis through its center: a solid cylinder or a hollow cylinder? Both cylinders have the same mass and radius.
a. Solid cylinder
b. Hollow cylinder
c. Both have same moment of inertia.
d. It depends on how quickly the cylinders are rolling.

27. Astronauts in orbit are sometimes considered to be "weightless." Consider the four propositions about *weightlessness* and determine which ones are true.
I. Weightlessness occurs in outer space because the force of gravity becomes negligible.
II. Weightlessness occurs when a ski jumper makes a jump.
III. Weightlessness occurs when you roll a baseball on the ground.
a. I only.
b. II only.
c. I and II.
d. I, II and III.

Copyright © Mometrix Media. You have been licensed one copy of this document for personal use only. Any other reproduction or redistribution is strictly prohibited. All rights reserved.

28. Two cars driving in opposite directions collide. If you ignore friction and any other outside interactions, which of the following statements is always true?
    a. The total momentum is conserved.
    b. The sum of the potential and kinetic energy are conserved.
    c. The total velocity of the cars is conserved.
    d. The total impulse is conserved.

29. Impulse is measured as the change in an object's momentum. Which statement is correct about the impulse on a ball rolling down a hill? Ignore air resistance and friction.
    a. The impulse is constant.
    b. The impulse only exists for a short time.
    c. The units of impulse are joules per second.
    d. The object's impulse increases.

30. Suppose a moving railroad car collides with an identical stationary car and the two cars latch together. Ignoring friction, and assuming no deformation on impact, which of the following statements is true?
    a. The speed of the first car decreases by half.
    b. The collision is elastic.
    c. The speed of the first car is doubled.
    d. There is no determining the final speed because the collision was inelastic.

31. A bowling ball with a mass of 4 kilograms moving at a speed of 10 meters per second hits a stationary 1 kg bowling ball in a head-on elastic collision. What is the speed of the stationary ball after the collision?
    a. 0 m/s
    b. 10 m/s.
    c. Less than 10 m/s, but not 0 m/s.
    d. More than 10 m/s

32. A 75-kg ice skater moving eastward at 5 m/s collides with a 100-kg skater moving northward at 4 m/s. Anticipating the collision, they hug each other and produce an inelastic collision. What is their final speed?
    a. Can't be determined from the information given.
    b. 3.1 m/s
    c. 4.1 m/s
    d. 2.1 m/s

33. A teacher pulls a box across the floor at a uniform speed. He pulls it with a spring scale showing that the force of kinetic friction is 2 newtons. How much total work is done in moving the box 5 meters?
    a. 0 joules
    b. 0.4 joules
    c. 10 joules
    d. 20 joules

Copyright © Mometrix Media. You have been licensed one copy of this document for personal use only. Any other reproduction or redistribution is strictly prohibited. All rights reserved.

34. Which statement best explains why the work done by a gravitational force on an object does not depend on the path the object takes.
   a. Work depends on the path when there is friction. The longer the path the more energy is required to overcome friction.
   b. Gravitational fields that arise from the interaction between point masses always produce elliptical paths of motion.
   c. A falling object experiences a change in potential energy.
   d. When an object falls down the work done by gravity is positive and when an object is thrown up the work done by gravity is negative.

35. Which statement correctly states the work-energy theorem?
   a. The change in kinetic energy of an object is equal to the work done by the object.
   b. The change in kinetic energy of an object is equal to the work done on an object.
   c. The change in potential energy of an object is equal to the work done by the object.
   d. The change in potential energy of an object is equal to the work done on an object.

36. An athlete's foot is in contact with a kicked football for 100 milliseconds and exerts a force on the football over a distance of 20 centimeters. The force starts at 0 N and increases linearly to 2000 N for 50 milliseconds through a distance of 10 centimeters and then decreases linearly for 50 milliseconds through a distance of 10 centimeters. What is the average power of the athlete's foot while it is in contact with the ball?

   a. 2 kilowatts
   b. 4 kilowatts
   c. 2000 kilowatts
   d. 4000 kilowatts

37. A motorcycle weighs twice as much as a bicycle and is moving twice as fast. Which of the following statements is true?
   a. The motorcycle has four times as much kinetic energy as the bicycle.
   b. The motorcycle has eight times as much kinetic energy as the bicycle.
   c. The bicycle and the motorcycle have the same kinetic energy.
   d. The bicycle has four times as much kinetic energy as the motorcycle.

- 74 -

Copyright © Mometrix Media. You have been licensed one copy of this document for personal use only. Any other reproduction or redistribution is strictly prohibited. All rights reserved.

38. A ball is released from a certain height along a frictionless track that does a loop-the-loop. The loop-the-loop part of the track is a perfect circle of radius R. At what height above the ground must the ball be released from in order to not fall off the track when it gets to the top of the loop-the-loop?

a. R
b. $2R$
c. $\dfrac{5R}{2}$
d. $3R$

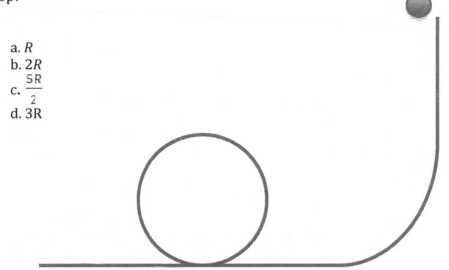

39. The potential energy of a spring is represented as $\frac{1}{2}kx^2$, where k represents the spring constant and x is the displacement of the spring from its position when it is not stretched. A massless spring is suspended from a support and a 100-g mass is attached, stretching it 2 centimeters. If another 100-g mass is attached, what is the new potential energy of the spring?
    a. Half as much as with one 100-g mass attached.
    b. One-forth as much as with one 100-g mass attached.
    c. Twice as much as with one 100-g mass attached.
    d. Four times as much as with one 100-g mass attached.

40. Two objects of masses m and M are a distance R apart. The force of their gravitational attraction is given by GmM/R^2. Their gravitational potential energy is given by $-GmM/R$. If the distance between these two objects doubles from 100 km to 200 km, what happens to the ratio of the gravitational force to the gravitational potential energy?
    a. Doubled
    b. Quadrupled
    c. Halved
    d. Quartered

41. Which of the following statements about energy is true?
    a. Mechanical energy is always conserved in an isolated system.
    b. Total energy is always conserved in an isolated system.
    c. Energy is never created or destroyed.
    d. You can determine the mechanical energy of an object by using the equation $E = mc^2$

Copyright © Mometrix Media. You have been licensed one copy of this document for personal use only. Any other reproduction or redistribution is strictly prohibited. All rights reserved.

42. Conservative forces are forces that do not lose energy to processes like friction and radiation and where the total mechanical energy is conserved. Which statement best explains why the work done by a conservative force on an object does not depend on the path the object takes?

    a. This is the definition of a conservative force.

    b. The work done by the force of friction on an object depends on the distance the object moves.

    c. Work can be positive, negative, or zero.

    d. If a force is conservative, any component of the force is equal to the change in a potential energy divided by the change in position.

43. How much does it cost to operate a 5 kilowatt electric motor for 12 hours if electricity is 6 cents per kilowatt-hour?

    a. $0.025

    b. $3.60

    c. $14.40

    d. $360

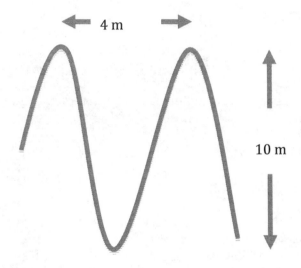

44. What is the wavelength in the above diagram?

    a. 2 meters

    b. 4 meters

    c. 5 meters

    d. 10 meters

45. Which of the following statements best explains what is meant by the phase of a wave?

    a. The height of a wave in 2π radians.

    b. The length of a wave in 2π radians.

    c. The period of oscillation of a wave.

    d. An angle indicating the wave cycle's instantaneous location.

Copyright © Mometrix Media. You have been licensed one copy of this document for personal use only. Any other reproduction or redistribution is strictly prohibited. All rights reserved.

46. A 100-kg bungee jumper jumps off a bridge, attached to a 20 meter bungee cord. After bouncing around for a minute he finally comes to rest. The stretched cord is now 25 meters long. What is the spring constant of the bungee cord?
   a. 20 newtons per meter
   b. 39 newtons per meter
   c. 49 newtons per meter
   d. 196 newtons per meter

47. The equation for the amplitude of the motion of an object undergoing simple harmonic motion is Asin[(5.0 Hz)t]. Assuming the wave's phase is measured in radians, what is the period of the motion?
   a. Sin [(5.0 Hz)t]
   b. 2.5 seconds
   c. 1.26 seconds
   d. A

48. Which of the following statements is true about the acceleration of a simple pendulum?
   a. The acceleration is constant.
   b. The magnitude of the acceleration is at a maximum when the bob is at the bottom of the path.
   c. The magnitude of the acceleration is at a maximum when the bob is changing directions.
   d. None of the above.

49. A RADAR gun sends out a pulsed beam of microwave radiation to measure the speed of cars using the Doppler effect. The pulsed beam bounces off the moving car and returns to the RADAR gun. For a car that's moving away from the RADAR detector, which of the following statements about the pulsed beam are true?
I. It returns with a longer wavelength.
II. It returns with a shorter wavelength.
III. It returns with a higher frequency.
   a. I only.
   b. II only.
   c. I and III.
   d. II and III.

50. What is the speed of a wave with a frequency of 12 Hz and a wavelength of 3 meters?
   a. 12 meters per second
   b. 36 meters per second
   c. 4 meters per second
   d. 0.25 meters per second

51. Two waves, each of which has an amplitude of A, cross paths. At the point where they cross, the peak of one wave meets the trough of another wave. What is the resulting amplitude at the point where the waves cross?
   a. 0
   b. A
   c. 2A
   d. –A

- 77 -

Copyright © Mometrix Media. You have been licensed one copy of this document for personal use only. Any other reproduction or redistribution is strictly prohibited. All rights reserved.

52. In resonance, small vibrations can produce a larger standing wave that becomes stronger than the original vibrations, assuming the vibrations are at the right frequency to generate resonance. If a pendulum is vibrated at a resonance frequency, what would you expect to happen?
    a. The period of the pendulum will increase.
    b. The time between swings will decrease.
    c. The pendulum will swing higher.
    d. The length of the pendulum will decrease.

53. Transverse travelling waves propagate through a taut string of length 20 meters at a speed of 4 m/s. Standing waves are set up in this string which is fixed at both ends. What is the smallest frequency possible for the standing waves?
    a. 0.1 Hz
    b. 0.05 Hz
    c. 0.2 Hz
    d. 0.4 Hz

54. Two tuning forks have a frequency of 500 Hz and 504 Hz and the same amplitude. How much time is there between beats?
    a. 4 seconds
    b. 15 seconds
    c. 0.25 seconds
    d. 2 seconds

55. Which of the following statements about refraction is true?
    a. Refraction means a change in direction of the wave.
    b. The angle of reflection equals the angle of refraction.
    c. The frequency in a refracted wave changes.
    d. The phase of a refracted wave changes.

56. What corresponds to the amplitude of a sound wave?
    a. loudness
    b. pressure differential of fluctuations
    c. magnitude of motion of air molecules
    d. power

57. The density of helium is much lower than that of air. How does the speed of sound traveling through helium gas compare to the speed of sound in air?
    a. It is faster
    b. It is slower
    c. It is the same speed
    d. It cannot be determined without knowing their atomic masses

58. What property of a sound wave in air corresponds to the frequency of the sound?
    a. pitch
    b. high and low
    c. timbre
    d. overtones

Copyright © Mometrix Media. You have been licensed one copy of this document for personal use only. Any other reproduction or redistribution is strictly prohibited. All rights reserved.

59. In musical instruments with two open ends, the first harmonic fits one-half wave inside the tube. The second harmonic fits 1 full wave in the tube. The third harmonic fits 1.5 full waves in the tube. Etc. An organ pipe, open at both ends, has a length of 1.2 meters. What is the frequency of the third harmonic? The speed of sound is 340 meters per second.
   a. 142 Hz
   b. 284 Hz
   c. 425 Hz
   d. 568 Hz

60. The speed of a travelling wave in a stretched string is given by $\sqrt{T/\mu}$, where T is the tension in the string and μ is the mass per unit length. A 2 meter long stretched string with a mass of 0.010 kilograms is made to resonate with standing waves at 50 Hz. What tension in the string is needed to produce the fourth harmonic? (Note: the fourth harmonic fits 2 full waves into the length of the string).
   a. 12. 5 newtons
   b. 25 newtons
   c. 50 newtons
   d. 10,000 newtons

61. Ultrasound imaging, which is used for various medical procedures, including imaging pregnant women, is based on which of the following principles.
   a. Doppler effect
   b. Echolocation
   c. Infrasonic
   d. Resonance.

62. Substance A has a density of 5.0 kg/m³ and substance B has a density of 4.0 kg/m³. What is the ratio of volume A to volume B when the masses of the two substances are equal?
   a. 1.25
   b. 0.80
   c. 1.12
   d. 0.89

63. A submarine sits underwater at a constant depth of 50 meters. Which of the following is true about the submarine's buoyant force?
   a. It is 0 N
   b. It is greater than 0 N but less than the submarine's weight
   c. It is equal to the submarine's weight
   d. It is greater than the submarine's weight

64. A hydraulic lift needs to raise a 3.5×10^3 newton truck. The input piston has a diameter of 2.0 cm and the output piston has a diameter of 24 cm. What minimum force must be applied to the input piston?
   a. 24 N
   b. 292 N
   c. 42,000 N
   d. 504,000 N

Copyright © Mometrix Media. You have been licensed one copy of this document for personal use only. Any other reproduction or redistribution is strictly prohibited. All rights reserved.

65. The center of a circular aquarium window with a radius 1 meter is 14 meters below the surface. What is the force of the water at this depth pushing on this window? The density of water is 1000 kg/m³.
    a. 1.37×10^5 newtons
    b. 1.08×10^5 newtons
    c. 4.3×10^5 newtons
    d. 0 newtons

66. Suppose you have a pipe of length L and radius r, and a liquid with viscosity η. You also have a sensor to detect the liquid's flow rate, which measures the volume of liquid passing through the pipe per second. If you want to increase the flow rate of the pipe, what changes to L, r and η should you make? Assume that the pressure differential remains constant.
    a. Increase L, increase r, and decreases η
    b. Decrease L, increase r, and decreases η
    c. Decrease L, increase r, and increase η
    d. Increase L, decrease r, and decreases η

67. An incompressible ideal fluid is flowing through a pipe 5.0 cm in radius at a speed of 6.0 m/s. The pipe narrows to 3.0 cm. What is the speed of flow in the narrower section?
    a. 10 m/s
    b. 3.6 m/s
    c. 16.7 m/s
    d. Can't be determined from the given information.

68. The air passing over an airplane's wing is considered an irrotational fluid flow. Which of the following statements correctly describes the concept of irrotational fluid flow?
    a. The fluid flows in a straight line.
    b. All particles have the same velocity as they pass a particular point.
    c. A tiny paddle wheel placed in the fluid will rotate.
    d. The fluid does not have any rotating points, whirlpools or eddies.

69. A cube of aluminum is placed at the bottom of a deep ocean where the pressure is over 20 atmospheres. What happens to the density of the cube?
    a. It remains the same.
    b. It decreases slightly.
    c. It increases slightly.
    d. It becomes zero.

70. Which statement correctly describes the elastic limit of a metal rod?
    a. The elastic limit occurs when a deformed object will no longer return to its original shape.
    b. The elastic limit occurs when the rod breaks.
    c. The elastic limit occurs when the stress stops producing a strain.
    d. The elastic limit assumes that the forces between molecules in a metal act like springs.

Copyright © Mometrix Media. You have been licensed one copy of this document for personal use only. Any other reproduction or redistribution is strictly prohibited. All rights reserved.

Thermal expansion coefficient

71. Which statement best explains why water expands when it freezes?
    a. The coefficient of thermal expansion is negative.
    b. The average distance between the water molecules increases.
    c. The density of water is greater at higher temperatures.
    d. The internal energy of the water decreases.

72. A cube of a substance is 5 centimeters on each side. It is placed in a pressure chamber where the pressure on each surface is $3.0 \times 10^7 \, N/m^2$, causing the density of the cube increases by 0.01 %. Which of the following theories is used to describe this?
    a. Young's Modulus
    b. Shear Modulus
    c. Elastic modulus
    d. Bulk Modulus

73. An object with a net charge is brought into the vicinity of an object with a net charge of zero coulombs. Which statement describes the electrostatic force between the two objects?
    a. It is a repulsive force.
    b. It is an attractive force.
    c. There is no force.
    d. It is a perpendicular force.

74. What does it mean when someone says that electric charge is conserved?
    a. Like charges repel, and unlike charges attract.
    b. The net charge of an isolated system remains constant.
    c. Charges come from electrons and protons.
    d. Charge can never be created or destroyed.

75. Which of the following is the correct definition of a conductor?
    a. A metal wire in an electrical circuit.
    b. A material that contains moveable electric charges.
    c. A material that is not a semiconductor or insulator.
    d. Any device that allows electricity to flow.

76. A charge +2q is placed at the origin of a coordinate system and a charge of -q is placed at a distance d from the origin. How far from the origin must a third charge +q be placed so that the net force on it is 0 newtons?
    a. Less than d/2
    b. Between d/2 and d
    c. Between d and 2d
    d. Greater than 2d

Copyright © Mometrix Media. You have been licensed one copy of this document for personal use only. Any other reproduction or redistribution is strictly prohibited. All rights reserved.

77. Which of the following statements best describes the electric field shown below.

    a. The field is decreasing down.
    b. The field is decreasing to the right.
    c. The field is increasing to the right.
    d. The field is uniform.

78. Which of the following statements about a solid metal sphere with a net charge is true?
    a. If the charge is positive it will be distributed uniformly throughout the sphere.
    b. The charge will be distributed uniformly at the surface of the sphere.
    c. The charge will leave the sphere.
    d. The electric field will be tangent to the surface of the sphere.

79. An electron moves in a uniform electric field in the same direction as the electric field from point A to point B. Which of the following statements is true?
    a. The potential energy of the electron decreased
    b. The potential energy of the electron increased
    c. The potential energy of the electron remained constant
    d. The potential energy of the electron was converted into kinetic energy

80. Which of the following is true of an electric dipole?
    a. They don't exist in nature.
    b. The charges are equal in magnitude and both are negative.
    c. The charges have opposite signs and can be unequal in magnitude.
    d. The charges are equal in magnitude and have opposite signs.

81. An electric field is pointing from south to north. If a dipole is placed in the field, how will the dipole's orientation change?
    a. The positive charge will be on the northern side and the negative charge will be on the southern side.
    b. The positive charge will be on the southern side and the negative charge will be on the northern side.
    c. The positive charge will be on the eastern side and the negative charge will be on the western side.
    d. There will be no change in the orientation.

82. When is the potential of a point charge with respect to a dipole equal to 0 volts per coulomb?
    a. At the midpoint between the positive and negative charge.
    b. At an infinite distance from the dipole.
    c. At the negative charge.
    d. At the positive charge.

Copyright © Mometrix Media. You have been licensed one copy of this document for personal use only. Any other reproduction or redistribution is strictly prohibited. All rights reserved.

83. A plastic comb is used to comb someone's dry hair and acquires a large positive charge. The comb is brought close to a small bit of uncharged paper lying on a table. Against the force of gravity, the bit of paper jumps up and sticks to the comb. What is likely to happen next?
    a. The paper will stick to the comb indefinitely.
    b. Air will eventually cause the comb to lose its charge and the paper will fall from the comb under the force of gravity.
    c. The paper will acquire a positive charge and be repelled by the comb.
    d. The paper will acquire a negative charge and be repelled by the comb.

84. Which law says the number of electric field lines passing through an imaginary surface is proportional to the net charge inside the surface?
    a. Coulomb's law
    b. Gauss's law
    c. Faraday's law of induction
    d. Biot-Savart law

85. The charged particle moving through a magnetic field will be subject to a force of $F = qvB \sin\theta$, where q is the charge, v is the particle's velocity, B is the magnetic field strength, and θ is the particle's angle between the magnetic field vector and the velocity vector. Charged particles from space enter the earth's atmosphere all the time. For example, the Aurora Borealis or Northern Lights are created by positive and negative charges passing through the Earth's magnetic field. Assume a proton with a speed of 8.0×10^6 meters per second enters the Earth's magnetic field at an angle of 45°, at a point where the magnetic field is 0.5 Teslas. What is the magnetic force acting on the proton? Note: the proton has a charge of 1.6×10^{-19} coulombs.
    a. 6.4×10^{-17} newtons
    b. 4.5×10^{-17} newtons
    c. 4.5×10^{-13} newtons
    d. 5.5×10^{-17} tesla

86. A magnetic field is directed into this page and an electron is moving from left to right as indicated in the diagram below.

x x x x x x
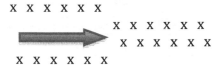
x x x x x x

In which direction will the electron move when it enters the magnetic field?
    a. It will curve upward.
    b. It will curve downward.
    c. It will curve in the direction of the magnetic field.
    d. It will curve in the direction opposite the magnetic field.

Copyright © Mometrix Media. You have been licensed one copy of this document for personal use only. Any other reproduction or redistribution is strictly prohibited. All rights reserved.

87. An electron is moving in a straight line. Another particle is moving in a straight line parallel to the path of the electron but in the opposite direction. Initially the electron and particle are far apart, but get closer together. When the two particles are in the vicinity of one another, they experience an attractive magnetic force. Which of the following is a correct inference from this fact?
    a. The particle has a north pole and a south pole.
    b. The particle is positively charged.
    c. The particle is negatively charged.
    d. The particle has either a north pole or a south pole.

88. A solenoid is made of loops of wire, through which a current is run. What is the purpose of putting a lot of loops into a solenoid?
    a. To increase the magnetic field inside the solenoid.
    b. To increate the magnetic field outside the solenoid.
    c. To decrease the magnetic field inside the solenoid.
    d. To decrease the magnetic field outside the solenoid.

89. In the 19th century, James Clerk Maxwell calculated the speed of light in a vacuum from the proportionality constants used in electrostatics and magnetism. Which of the following relationships correctly identifies how light moves in a vacuum?
    a. High frequencies of light travel faster than low frequencies.
    b. Low frequencies of light travel faster than high frequencies.
    c. All frequencies of light travel at the same speed in a vacuum.
    d. Light moves at infinite speed through a vacuum.

90. Electromagnetic radiation — also known as light — consists of perpendicularly oscillating electric and magnetic fields. Which of the following statements about electromagnetic radiation is untrue?
    a The energy of the radiation is determined by the frequency and Plank's constant.
    b. The "color" of light is determined by its wavelength.
    c. Electromagnetic radiation sometimes obeys wave theory.
    d. Electromagnetic radiation sometimes obeys particle theory.

91. Which of the following gives the correct order of electromagnetic radiation from the lowest frequency to the highest frequency?
    a. microwaves, UHF radio waves, x-rays, visible light
    b. UHF radio waves, visible light, microwaves, x-rays
    c. UHF radio waves, microwaves, visible light, x-rays
    d. microwaves, x-rays, visible light, UHF radio waves

Copyright © Mometrix Media. You have been licensed one copy of this document for personal use only. Any other reproduction or redistribution is strictly prohibited. All rights reserved.

92. The diagram below shows two batteries connected in series to a resistor. What is the direction of current flow?

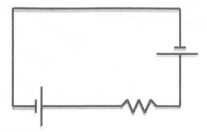

    a. clockwise
    b. counterclockwise
    c. neither clockwise nor counterclockwise
    d. Can't be determined from the information given.

93. Current in an electrical circuit is normally measured in amperes. Which of the following does not represent an alternative way of expressing units of current?
    a. coulombs per second
    b. volts per ohm
    c. electrons per second
    d. Watt-volts.

94. Which of the following devices changes chemical energy into electrical energy?
    a. battery
    b. closed electric circuit
    c. generator
    d. transformer

95. Which of the following statements about electricity flowing through a circuit can be correctly derived from Ohm's law?
    a. Increasing the voltage decreases the current if the resistance remains unchanged.
    b. Increasing the current and the resistance decreases the voltage.
    c. Increasing the current increases the voltage if the resistance is unchanged.
    d. Increasing the resistance increases the current if the voltage remains unchanged.

96. A circuit consists of a battery and a resistor. An ammeter is used to measure the current in the circuit and is connected in series to the circuit. Which of the following is true?
    a. The current flowing in the resistor increases.
    b. The current flowing in the resistor decreases.
    c. The voltage drop across the resistor increases.
    d. The current flowing in the resistor remains the same.

Copyright © Mometrix Media. You have been licensed one copy of this document for personal use only. Any other reproduction or redistribution is strictly prohibited. All rights reserved.

97. What is the total resistance between points X and Y in the circuit diagram below?

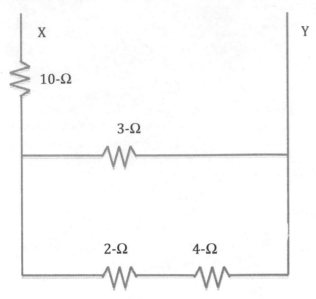

a. 0 Ω
b. 12 Ω
c. 19 Ω
d. 16 Ω

98. Consider one tungsten wire of length L and cross-sectional area A and another tungsten wire of length $2L$ and area $2A$. Assuming both wires are the same temperature, which of the following statements is true?
    a. The resistance of the two wires is the same.
    b. The resistance of the longer wire is twice the resistance of the shorter wire.
    c. The resistance of the longer wire is half the resistance of the shorter wire.
    d. The resistance of the longer wire is four times the resistance of the shorter wire.

99. A capacitor is connected in series to a battery and a resistor. The battery is disconnected after the capacitor is charged and replaced by a battery with a greater electromotive force, causing the capacitor to gain additional charge. After the capacitor has fully charged again, which of the following statements is true about the capacitance of the circuit?
    a. It has increased.
    b. It has decreased.
    c. It has remained the same.
    d. It has become zero.

Copyright © Mometrix Media. You have been licensed one copy of this document for personal use only. Any other reproduction or redistribution is strictly prohibited. All rights reserved.

100. Which is the correct formula for the energy stored in a fully-charged capacitor with capacitance C when its attached to a battery of voltage V?
    a. C/V
    b. ½CV²
    c. CV
    d. 0 volt

101. Adding multiple capacitors to a circuit is much the opposite as adding multiple resistors. Adding resistors in series, for example, creates an effective resistance equal to their sum. To add resistors in parallel, you must add the reciprocals of their resistance. With capacitors, however, you use reciprocals when adding them in series and you sum the capacitance when adding in parallel. Given the following diagram, what is the total capacitance of the circuit?

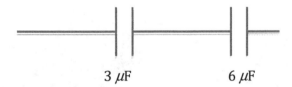

    3 μF   6 μF

    a. 2-microfarads
    b. 9-microfarads
    c. 0.5-microfarads
    d. 4.5 microfarads

102. A 5-microfarad and a 15-microfarad capacitor are connected as shown in the diagram. What is the total capacitance of the circuit?

5 μF

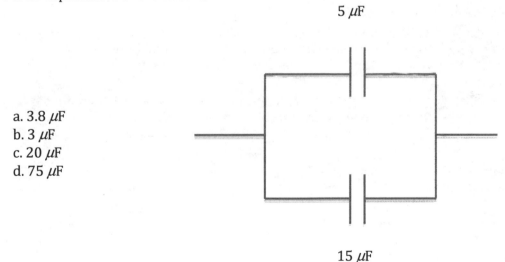

    a. 3.8 μF
    b. 3 μF
    c. 20 μF
    d. 75 μF

15 μF

Copyright © Mometrix Media. You have been licensed one copy of this document for personal use only. Any other reproduction or redistribution is strictly prohibited. All rights reserved.

103. A 6.0-megaohm resistor is connected in series with a 5.0-microfarad capacitor and fully charged with a 3-volt battery. The battery is disconnected and the capacitor is connected directly to the resistor. How long will it take for the capacitor to fully discharge?
   a. Infinite time
   b. 30 seconds
   c. 0.0333 second
   d. 90 seconds

104. A miniature heater has a power rating of 50 watts and is connected to a battery with an electromotive force of 10 volts. What current flows through the heater?
   a. 500 amperes
   b. 5 amperes
   c. 200 milliamperes
   d. 3.1×10^{19} electrons per second

105. A homemade generator rotates at a constant frequency and produces an alternating current with a maximum voltage of 40 volts. It is connected to a resistor of 20 ohms. What is the average current that flows through the resistor?
   a. 0 amperes.
   b. 1.4 amperes
   c. 2.0 amperes
   d. 2.8 amperes

106. Two beams of light with the same phase and wavelength travel different paths and arrive at the same point. If maximum constructive interference occurs at this point, which of the following statements is true?
   a. The two beams arrive 180° out of phase.
   b. The two beans arrive 90° out of phase.
   c. The lengths of the paths differ by an odd-number of half wavelengths.
   d. The lengths of the paths differ by an integral number of wavelengths.

107. When light from a single source strikes two slits, alternating bright and dark lines appear on a screen on the far side. What is the best explanation for this phenomenon?
   a. Doppler shift
   b. Diffraction and interference
   c. Chromatic aberration
   d. Total internal reflection

108. Which of the following is true about a diffraction grating?
   a. The more slits per inch, the greater the amount of destructive interference.
   b. Blue light diffracts more than red light in a diffraction grating.
   c. A diffraction grating produces maxima and minima only for monochromatic light.
   d. Light passing through a diffraction grating produces a bulls-eye pattern.

Copyright © Mometrix Media. You have been licensed one copy of this document for personal use only. Any other reproduction or redistribution is strictly prohibited. All rights reserved.

109. Which of the following statements best explains why light is polarized?
    a. Light waves' electromagnetic fields can be oriented in a particular direction by a polarizer.
    b. Photons of light can be pointed in the same direction by microscopic holes in a polarizer.
    c. Light travels in a vacuum.
    d. Light is a longitudinal wave.

110. Which of the following phenomena implies that light consists of specific quanta?
    a. ultraviolet catastrophe
    b. threshold frequency
    c. emission of light
    d. stability of atoms

111. Which of the following phenomena is most closely related to the phenomenon that produces the light from lasers?
    a. radioactivity
    b. phosphorescence
    c. sunlight
    d. blackbody radiation

112. Specular reflection might occur on a surface like a mirror, while diffuse reflection might occur on a wooden tabletop. Which of the following statements best describes the difference between specular and diffuse reflection?
    a. For diffuse reflection, the angle of incidence is equal to the angle of reflection.
    b. For diffuse reflection, surface irregularities are large compared to the wavelength of visible light.
    c. One hundred percent of the light is reflected for specular reflection.
    d. The conservation of momentum is followed in specular reflection.

113. A ray of light travelling in a vacuum (n = 1) is incident upon a glass plate (n = 1.3). It hits with an angle of incidence of 45°. If the angle of incidence increases to 50°, what is the new angle of refraction?
    a. It is 45°
    b. It is 50°
    c. It is below 45°
    d. It is above 50°

114. Which of the following statements explains what causes a rainbow?
    a. The components of sunlight strike water droplets at different angles.
    b. Water molecules produce an emission spectrum when sunlight strikes them.
    c. The speed of light in water depends on its wavelength.
    d. There is total internal reflection for certain wavelengths of sunlight.

Copyright © Mometrix Media. You have been licensed one copy of this document for personal use only. Any other reproduction or redistribution is strictly prohibited. All rights reserved.

115. Which of the following theories best explains the phenomenon of total internal reflection?
  a. The speed of light is a maximum in a vacuum.
  b. Light consists of bundles of energy called photons.
  c. Snell's law places a limit on the angle of refraction.
  d. Light consists of transverse waves.

116. Two rays parallel to the optical axis of a concave mirror are incident upon the mirror. Where do the two rays intersect?
  a. At a point behind the mirror.
  b. At infinity.
  c. At the center of curvature.
  d. At the focal point.

117. An object is placed a certain distance away from a convex spherical mirror. Which of the following statements is true?
  a. No image is formed.
  b. The image will be larger or smaller, depending on the object's distance from the mirror.
  c. The image will be smaller and right side up.
  d. The image will be smaller and either right side up or upside down, depending on the object's distance from the mirror.

118. Which of the following statements about the image created by a magnifying glass is true?
  a. The image is always upside down.
  b. The image is always right side up.
  c. The image may be right side up or upside down, depending on the location of the object.
  d. The image may be right side up or upside down, depending on the thickness of the lens.

119. An object is 20 cm in front of a thin convex lens with a focal point of 10 cm. Where is the image located?
  a. 10 cm in front of the lens.
  b. 20 cm in front of the lens.
  c. 10 cm behind the lens.
  d. 20 cm behind the lens.

120. A lens forms an upright image 19 cm from a lens of an object 49 cm from the lens. The object and image are on the same side of the lens. What is the magnification of the image?
  a. 0.39
  b. 2.6
  c. 13.7
  d. 31.2

Copyright © Mometrix Media. You have been licensed one copy of this document for personal use only. Any other reproduction or redistribution is strictly prohibited. All rights reserved.

121. A thin convex lens has focal length of 30 cm. An identical lens is placed right behind it. What is the focal length of this combination of lenses?
   a. 30 cm.
   b. 60 cm
   c. 15 cm
   d. 0.067 cm

122. Which type of aberration does not occur with concave spherical mirrors?
   a. Astigmatism
   b. Chromatic aberration
   c. Spherical aberration
   d. Distortion

123. Which of the following statements is not a principle used in constructing ray diagrams to show the creation of images using a thin convex lens?
   a. A ray parallel to the optical axis is refracted so that it goes through the focal point of the lens.
   b. A ray that goes through the focal point of a lens and strikes the lens is refracted parallel to the optical axis.
   c. A ray that goes through the center of a lens is not deflected.
   d. A ray that strikes the surface of a lens follows Snell's law for refraction.

124. What is the magnification of a combination of three lenses with magnifications 3.0, −4.0, and 0.3?
   a. − 0.7
   b. 0.7
   c. − 3.6
   d. 3.6

125. A hydrogen atom makes a transition from the first excited state to the ground level. Which of the following statements is true?
   a. A 10.2 eV photon is emitted.
   b. A 13.6 eV photon is emitted.
   c. A 1.9 eV photon is absorbed.
   d. No photon is emitted.

126. A substance has a half-life of 2.4×10^4 years. How long does it take for 87.5% of the substance to decay?
   a. 2.1×10^4 years
   b. 4.5×10^4 years
   c. 7.2×10^4 years
   d. 9.6×10^4 years

127. A nucleus absorbs a neutron and undergoes a fission reaction. Which of the following statements explains why this happens?
   a. The nucleus is more stable with the additional neutron.
   b. The new nucleus is unstable.
   c. Energy is released.
   d. The binding energy per nucleon decreases.

Copyright © Mometrix Media. You have been licensed one copy of this document for personal use only. Any other reproduction or redistribution is strictly prohibited. All rights reserved.

128. How is light created in the core of the sun?
    a. convection
    b. fission reactions
    c. fusion reactions
    d. chemical reactions

129. How is energy generated in a nuclear reaction?
    a. Matter is converted into energy.
    b. Photon excitation and emission.
    c. Kinetic collision of highly energetic hydrogen atoms.
    d. Gravitational energy is converted into electromagnetic radiation.

130. Which of the following statements about isotopes of an element is true?
    a. They have the same number of nucleons.
    b. They have the same number of neutrons, but different numbers of protons.
    c. They have the same number of protons, but different numbers of neutrons.
    d. They have a different number of electrons.

131. What happens to a nucleus when it emits an alpha particle?
    a. Its atomic number decreases by one.
    b. Its mass decreases by two atomic mass units.
    c. Its nucleon number decreases by four.
    d. Its charge increases by +2.

132. Cobalt-63 can be produced in a laboratory and is unstable. When it decays, a neutron in its core will likely decay into a proton, changing Cobalt-63 into Nickel-63. Which of the following products will be produced when a neutron decays into a proton?
I. alpha particles
II. beta particle
III. gamma particles
    a. I only
    b. III only
    c. II and III
    d. I, II and III

133. An inch is approximately equivalent to which of the following?
    a. 25.4 mm
    b. 25.4 cm
    c. 2.54×10^{-4} km
    d. 2.54×10^2 m

134. Which of the following numbers has the most significant digits?
    a. 1,500,000
    b. 1.5000×10^5
    c. 0.15000
    d. 0.00150000

Copyright © Mometrix Media. You have been licensed one copy of this document for personal use only. Any other reproduction or redistribution is strictly prohibited. All rights reserved.

135. Suppose your actual weight is 150 pounds and you weigh yourself with an analog scale and get a reading of 152.1 pounds. You repeat the measurement twice more and get 152.1 pounds each time. Which of the following statements is true?

    a. There is no random error.
    b. There is no systematic error.
    c. The systematic error is 2.1 pounds.
    d. The random error is 2.1 pounds.

136. A school nurse measures the height of every boy in a school with 1000 pupils and determines that the average height is 1.64 meters with a standard deviation of 0.05 meter. Which of the following statements is true?

    a. Sixty-eight percent of the students have heights between 1.59 meters and 1.69 meters.
    b. There are as many students with heights above 1.64 meters as below 1.64 meters.
    c. More students are 1.64 meters tall than any other height.
    d. None of these statements may be made conclusively.

Copyright © Mometrix Media. You have been licensed one copy of this document for personal use only. Any other reproduction or redistribution is strictly prohibited. All rights reserved.

Answers and Explanations

1. B: Significant digits indicate the precision of the measurement. Answer B has 5 significant figures. A and C each have 4. D has 3. The leading zeros in Answers A and D and are not counted as significant digits, but zeros at the end of the number (as in Answers A and B) do count. In answer D, the zero in between 2 and 9 is significant.

2. D: When adding, the answer will have as many significant figures after the decimal point as the measurement with the fewest decimal places. The total mass (ignoring significant figure) is obtained by adding up all four measurements. This yields B, not A. But since the first and second masses are precise to only a hundredth of a gram, your answer can't be more precise than this. The number 35.5918, when rounded to two significant figures after the decimal point (to match your measurement of 23.04) is 35.59.

3. C: Vectors have a magnitude (e.g., 5 meters/second) and direction (e.g., towards north). Of the choice listed, only velocity has a direction. (35 m/s north, for example). Speed, distance and time are all quantities that have a size but not a direction. That's why, for example, a car's speedometer reads 35 miles/hour, but does not indicate your direction of travel.

4. C: Displacement is a vector that indicates the change in the location of an object. Answer A would be correct if the question asked for the total distance the person walked or if the person didn't change direction. If the person turned around $180°$, the displacement could be as small as 5 meters. If the person changed directions only a fraction of a degree, its magnitude would be *less* than 13 meters, not as *large* as 13 meters.

5. C: To add and subtract vectors algebraically, you add and subtract their components. To add vectors graphically, you shift the location of the vectors so that they are connected tail-to-tail. The resultant is a vector that starts at the tail of the first vector and ends at the tip of the second. To subtract vectors, however, you connect the vectors tail-to-tail, not tip to tail, starting with the vector that is not subtracted, and ending with the one that is. Think of this just like vector addition, except the vector that is subtracted (the one with the negative sign in front of it) switches directions.

6. C: The average speed is the total distance (400 m) divided by the total time spent travelling (100 s). Answer A would be correct if the question asked for the instantaneous velocity while the runner was stopped. Ans. B is the runner's average speed when running at her usual time, finishing the race in 80 seconds. Answer D is the average speed if the runner had completed the race in 20 seconds, not 100.

7. B: The answer can be determined because the rate of acceleration is uniform. Since the acceleration is 5 m/s^2, the velocity increases by 5 m/s every second. If it starts at 20 m/s, after 1 second it will be going 25 m/s. After another second it will be going 30 m/s, so the total time is 2 seconds. You can also calculate this time by using the average speed. Since the object undergoes uniform acceleration, the average speed is 25 m/s. Using the distance traveled, the same result is obtained. t = d / v = 50 meters / 25 m/s = 2 seconds.

Copyright © Mometrix Media. You have been licensed one copy of this document for personal use only. Any other reproduction or redistribution is strictly prohibited. All rights reserved.

8. C: This is a problem of free-fall in two-dimensions. A thrown ball without air resistance will only be subjected to one force, gravity. This causes a downward acceleration of exactly 9.8 m/s² on all objects, regardless of their size, speed or position. Note: since the ball was thrown directly upwards, the HORIZONTAL acceleration is 0 m/s² and the horizontal speed at all times is 0 m/s. B is wrong because the force of gravity is always pointed downward and never changes direction.

9. C: In a uniform gravitational field, such as occurs near Earth's surface, an object will move like a point mass located at the center of mass. However, this does not necessarily mean that the geometrical center of an object is the same as its center of mass, depending on its shape, design and mass distribution. The center of mass of a sphere or cube is at its geometric center because you can imagine the sphere as consisting of a large number of point masses located at certain points in space. Multiplying the point masses by their location and dividing by the total mass gives the center of mass. I is not true because the space station may not be completely symmetrical. III is true because the space station is undergoing uniform circular motion around Earth. If the orbit had been elliptical, this would not be true because the speed would have changed depending on the station's position. However, even though the speed is constant in a circular orbit, the velocity is not. Since velocity has a direction associated with it, and the space station is moving in a circular path, its velocity is constantly changing.

10. A: Newton's first law (inertia) says an object in motion stays in motion, and an object at rest stays at rest, unless external forces act on them. I is an excellent demonstration because it shows the ball at rest and in motion. At rest, the ball stays at rest until a force acts on it. When the ball is moving, there is no force acting on the ball in the direction of motion. Thus, the natural state of the ball is to be at rest or moving with a constant speed. Ans. C is not a good demonstration because the force of friction is what makes it hard to move the heavy object. Ans B is a good demonstration of equilibrium and friction. Ans D, running a current through wires, has nothing to do with Newton's first law.

11. B: The newton is defined in terms of the fundamental units meters, kilograms, and seconds (N = kg × m/s²), so it is not a fundamental unit. II is a verbal statement of $F = ma$, Newton's second law, which is true. If $F = 0$ N, then the acceleration is 0 m/s². If the acceleration is 0 m/s², then the speed is 0 m/s or a nonzero constant. This is a nonverbal statement of Newton's first law, meaning Newton's first law can be derived from his second law. Newton's second law cannot be derived from the universal law of gravity.

12. A: Newton's third law is that if object A exerts a force on object B, then object B exerts and equal and opposite force on object A. This means for every action (force) there is a reaction (force in opposite direction). The box is in equilibrium because the force of the table on the box is equal and opposite to the force of gravity (weight) of the box pushing against the table. Since the force of the box against the table is an action force (caused by gravity), the reaction force would be the table pushing back against the box.

13. D: There will be a gravitational force of attraction between the two spheres determined by the universal constant of gravity, the distance between the spheres, and the mass of the spheres. Since both objects are affected by this force (remember, Newton's 3rd law says the force needs to be equal and opposite), both objects will experience a slight acceleration and start moving towards each other a tiny amount (when we ignore friction). Using F = ma, you know that the less massive sphere will experience a larger acceleration than the more massive one.

Copyright © Mometrix Media. You have been licensed one copy of this document for personal use only. Any other reproduction or redistribution is strictly prohibited. All rights reserved.

14. C: The centripetal force pushes you in toward the center of the ring, not towards the wall. The centripetal force also causes the ring to push against you, which is why it might feel like you're being push outwards. This force also causes friction between your back and the wall, and that's why you don't fall when the floor is removed, assuming the frictional force is large enough to overcome gravity. As the speed of rotation increases, the force exerted by the wall on your body increases, so the frictional force between you and the wall increases. Answer B is correct—centripetal force does cause you to change direction—but it does not explain why you don't fall. Also note that "centrifugal force" is an illusion; because you feel the wall pushing against your back, you feel like you're being pushed outwards. In fact, you're being pulled inwards, but the wall is also being pulled inwards and is pushing against you. Finally, you are not weightless on a ride like this.

15. C: Centripetal force can be expressed as $F = m(v^2/r)\cos\theta$. Increasing the radius effectively decreases the force unless you also increase the velocity. By assuming that the maximum centripetal force remains constant, you can increase the maximum speed v by as much as $\sqrt{2}$. Any higher and the v^2 term will be too high for the new radius.

16. C: The weight of an object near Earth's surface is given by $W = mg$, where g = 9.8 m/s². The Earth exerts a force on the 10 kg object equal 10 kg x 9.8 m/s²= 98 N. This weight pulls on the lower spring, stretching it until it reads 98 N. The lower spring then exerts a force of 98 N on the upper spring, causing it to read 98 N.

17. C: The question asks how much friction is needed to START the block moving, which means you need to calculate the force of static friction. If the question had asked about the force needed to KEEP the object moving at a constant speed, you would calculate the force of kinetic friction. Here, the force of static friction is equal to $\mu_{static} \times N$, where N is the Normal force. The normal force (N) on the plastic block is the weight of the block (mg) = 10 kg x 9.8 m/s² = 98 newtons. The force of static friction = 0.6 x 98N = 59 N. Answer B is the force of kinetic friction, once the block starts moving. (Note: molecular bonding and abrasion cause friction. When the surfaces are in motion the bonding is less strong, so the coefficient of kinetic friction is less than the coefficient of static friction. Therefore, more force is required to start the box moving than to keep it moving.)

18. A: The force of gravity points straight down. The normal force is perpendicular to the surface of the block. The force of friction points down the slope. The only one of these diagrams with all three vectors pointing in those directions is Answer A.

19. B: The ideal mechanical advantage (IMA) of a simple machine ignores friction. It is the effort force divided into the resultant force. It is also the distance the effort force moves divided by the distance the resultant force moves. The IMA of a fixed pulley is 1 because all a fixed pulley does is change the direction of the effort force. A moveable pulley, however, doubles the force by increasing the distance by two. In this case, there is one fixed pulley and one floating pulley. Since the IMA of the fixed pulley is 1, and the floating pulley doubles this, the total IMA is 2.

20. B: The weight of the masses is determined from $W = mg$. In this case, there is a force to the left/down of 20 kg x 9.8 m/s² = 196 N, and a force to the right/down of 30 kg x 9.8 m/s² = 294 N. The net force is 98 N to the right/down. This force is moving both masses, however, which have a total mass of 50 kg. Using F = ma and solving for acceleration gives a = 98 N / 50 kg = 2 m/s².

Copyright © Mometrix Media. You have been licensed one copy of this document for personal use only. Any other reproduction or redistribution is strictly prohibited. All rights reserved.

21. B: Using Newton's second law F = ma, the acceleration of all three blocks, which have a combined mass of 9 kg, is a = 25 N / 9 kg = 2.78 m/s². The force pulling the rear block is F = ma = 4 kg x 2.78 m/s² = 11.1 N. Another way of thinking of this is the tension represents 4/9 of the total force, since the total mass is 9 kg and the rear block has a mass of 4 kg. This must equal the tension on the rope pulling on that block. Answer C is the tension of the string connecting the 3 kg and 2 kg masses. Answer D is the tension on the rope pulling all 3 masses.

22. D: The weight of the art is 200 kg x 9.8 m/s² = 1960 N. This is the total force pulling DOWN on the wires. However, the tension acts along a 40° angle, and the vertical force is T sinθ. However there are two ends to the wire, which splits the tension, meaning the weight is spread across 2T sinθ. So 2T sinθ = w. Therefore, T = ½ x 1960 N / sin(40) = 1524 N. Note: There's also a horizontal component to the tension forces, each expressed as T cosθ. The net force of the left and right tensions is zero. Answer A is calculated using the Cos(40) instead of Sin(40).

23. B: The torque acting on an object is the force acting on the object (in this case, its weight = mg) times its distance from the pivot point. Here, the masses and the bar are balanced, so the net torque is 0 N × m. This means the clockwise torque is equal and opposite to the counter clockwise torque ($m_1 g d_1 = m_2 g d_2$). Dividing the distance in half would only add a factor of ½ to both sides of this equation. Since this affects both sides equally, the net torque is still zero when both distances are halved. C would be the correct answer if the mass of the bar was not zero.

24. B: Clockwise is the direction the hands of a clock rotate when looking at the clock, so a counterclockwise torque would require a force that pushes or pulls down on the lever. The pivot point is the axis of rotation. We don't care about the components of these forces that push either to the left or right, since these components do not produce any torque. Force 1 is directed into the axis, so it produces no torque. Forces 3 and 4 both push up on the lever. The only force producing a counter-clockwise rotation is Force 2.

25. C: All three laws are operating, but the third law (forces come in equal and opposite pairs) best explains the motion. The first law (inertia) is shown from the fact that the balloon doesn't move until a force acts upon it. The second law (F = ma) is shown because you can see the force and the acceleration. The force comes from the contraction of the rubber balloon. The stretched rubber exerts a force on the air inside the balloon. This causes the air to accelerate in accordance with the second law. You can't see this acceleration because the air is invisible and because it is all the air in the room that the balloon is exerting a force on. However, the air in the room exerts and equal and opposite force on the balloon (this is Newton's third law), which causes the balloon to accelerate in the direction it did.

26. B: The moment of inertia of a point mass about any axis is given by mR^2, where R is the distance from the axis. The moment of inertia of a solid object is calculated by imagining that the object is made up of point masses and adding the moments of inertia of the point masses. The average radius of the particles in a hollow cylinder will be R (all the mass is at radius R). For a solid cylinder, however, the average radius is less than R, meaning the overall moment of inertia will be smaller, which means Answer B is correct. To actually calculate the moment of inertia of a cylinder of thickness $R_2 - R_1$ is $\frac{1}{2} m (R_1^2 + R_2^2)$. For a solid cylinder, R_1 = 0 meters. For a hollow cylinder, $R_1 = R_2$.

Copyright © Mometrix Media. You have been licensed one copy of this document for personal use only. Any other reproduction or redistribution is strictly prohibited. All rights reserved.

27. B: The phenomenon known as weightlessness is caused by an object being in free fall. An object in space still experiences a gravitational force due to the earth, but if that object is in orbit, it's effectively free falling around the earth, which causes it to experience weightlessness. Here, proposition I is wrong because you have to be pretty far away from a star for gravity to become negligible. In fact, objects only stay in orbit because the earth's gravity pulls on them and causes them to change direction. This means the usual experience of weight is lost, as you can see by the floating objects and people inside an orbiting spaceship. The same thing happens to a ski jumper, who is in free fall after he or she jumps. If the jumper is carrying a rock, for example, that rock will feel weightless while the jumper is in the air. A rolled baseball is not in freefall and does not experience weightlessness.

28. A: In a closed system (when you ignore outside interactions), the total momentum is constant and conserved. The total energy would also be conserved, although not the sum of the potential and kinetic energy. Some of the energy from the collision would be turned into thermal energy (heat) for example. Nor is the total velocity conserved, even though the velocity is a component of the momentum, since the momentum also depends on the mass of the cars. The impulse is a force over time that causes the momentum of a body to change. It doesn't make sense to think of impulse as conserved, since it's not necessarily constant throughout a collision.

29. D: Impulse is the change in an object's momentum (mv), which is in units of kg x m/s. An object's impulse can change, depending on the forces acting upon it. For a ball rolling down a hill, gravity provides a constant force, which causes the ball to accelerate. This creates an impulse that increases as the ball gets faster and faster. This impulse does not exist for a short time, but will continue as long as the ball is accelerating.

30. A: A collision is considered elastic when neither object loses any kinetic energy. Since the cars latch together, this can't be the case. You could easily prove this by calculating the cars' KE = $\frac{1}{2}mv^2$. If the railroad cars had bumpers instead of couplers, the moving car would stop and transfer all its momentum and kinetic energy to the stationary car, causing an elastic collision. In a closed system like this one, however, the conservation of momentum is an absolute law, where an objects' momentum is its mass times its velocity. There are no external forces acting on the two cars. The only forces are between the two cars themselves. The momentum before the collision is the same as the momentum after the collision: $mv_{initial} + m(0 \text{ m/s}) = mv_{final} + mv_{final}$. So $mv_{initial} = 2mv_{final}$, and $v_{initial} = 2v_{final}$. Thus the final velocity is half the initial velocity.

31. D: Since this is a head-on elastic collision, you could use conservation of kinetic energy and momentum to actually solve this problem. However, in this case, you only need to think through the answers to arrive at a correct conclusion. Clearly the ball after it's struck won't be going 0 m/s. And since this is an elastic collision, and it is hit by a much larger ball, it must be going faster than the larger ball was originally moving. Therefore, the ball will be moving at more than 10 m/s. If this were an inelastic collision where the balls stuck together, the ball would final velocity would be less than 10 m/s.

32. B: Using conservation of momentum, the original eastward momentum = 75 x 5 = 375 kg m/s and the northward momentum is 100 x 4 = 400 kg m/s. Afterwards, the two skaters have a combined mass of 175 kg. Using the Pythagorean theorem (for a right triangle w/ hypotenuse A, $A^2 = B^2 + C^2$), their total momentum will be $\sqrt{(375^2 + 400^2)}$ = 548 KG M/S. Setting this equal to mv, 548 = (175) v, gives v = 3.1 m/s.

Copyright © Mometrix Media. You have been licensed one copy of this document for personal use only. Any other reproduction or redistribution is strictly prohibited. All rights reserved.

33. A: Since the box is moving at a uniform speed, the net force on the box is 0 newtons. Thus the work (W = Fd) is also 0 joules. Answer C incorrectly assumes that 2 newtons of force are used to move the box 5 meters, and while it's true that the teacher is pulling with 2 newtons, the frictional force counteracts this. Answer D incorrectly assumes the work performed by the teacher and the work due to friction add together for a net work of 20 newtons. Answer B incorrectly uses W = F/d. The vertical forces acting on the box—gravity and the normal force—also have a net force of 0 newtons and work of 0 joules.

34. C: To determine how much work is done by a gravitational force, you should calculate the change in that object's potential energy = mgh, where m = mass, g = the gravitational acceleration 9.8 m/s^2 and h = height. Therefore, the work done only depends on the change in height and not on the path taken. In Answer A, the work done by gravity doesn't have anything to do with friction, so this is not a good explanation. Friction is a separate force. Answer D, although true, doesn't explain why the work doesn't depend on the path.

35. B: The work-energy theorem can be written $W = \Delta KE$. It is derived from Newton's second law ($F = ma$) by multiplying both sides by the distance the object moves. This work is the work done by a force on an object, and not the work done by an object. Work is only done by an object if that object exerts a force on another object, causing a change in its kinetic energy or position. The work done on an object MAY equal its potential energy, but only if that potential energy is converted into kinetic energy. In real-life cases, some energy is converted to heat, for example, so the change in potential energy does not equal the change in kinetic energy.

36. A: In addition to understanding power, this problem requires you to understand unit conversions. The power P is the work divided by the time, and the work here is the average force times distance. Since the force increases evenly from 0 to 2000N and decreases at the same rate, the average force is 1000N. Keeping in mind that 20 cm = 0.2 m and 100 milliseconds = 0.1 seconds, this means P = 1000N x 0.2 m / 0.1 s = 2000 watts or 2 kilowatts.

37. B: Kinetic energy is the energy of motion and is defined as ½mv^2. Using this equation, if you double the mass and the velocity of an object, you find KE = ½(2m)(2v)^2 or 8 times the original KE. Therefore, the motorcycle has 8 times as much kinetic energy as the bicycle.

38. C: The initial gravitational potential energy of the ball is mgh, where h is the height above the ground. At the top of the loop, some of this energy will be converted into kinetic energy (½mv$_{top}^2$). Since its height is 2R at the top of the loop, it will have a potential energy here of $mg(2R)$. Using the conservation of energy: $mgh = ½m\,v_{top}^2 + mg(2R)$. Additionally, in order to maintain a circular path, the centripetal force must equal the gravitational force at the top of the loop: $\frac{(m\,v_{top}^2)}{R} = mg$, which can be rewritten as $v_{top}^2 = gR$. Putting this into the energy equation, you find $mgh = ½\,m(gR) + mg(2R)$. Dividing m and g from both sides of this equation shows that $h = ½R + 2R = \frac{5}{2}R$. Answers A, B and C represent choices that testess are likely to find if they do the math incorrectly.
PE = (1/2)kx^2(spring)

39. D: The formula for the potential energy of a spring comes from calculating how much work is required to stretch a spring an amount x. Hooke's law applies so the force increases uniformly from 0 N to kx, where k is the spring constant. Hence, $PE = ½kx^2$. There are two ways to solve this problem. If you recognize that doubling the mass will double how much the spring is stretched, you can easily see that (2x)^2 shows the potential energy of the spring quadruples. If you don't realize

Copyright © Mometrix Media. You have been licensed one copy of this document for personal use only. Any other reproduction or redistribution is strictly prohibited. All rights reserved.

that the displacement doubles, you can easily prove it, since F = ma = -kx for a spring. Doubling the mass would double the force, and thereby double the displacement x. The spring constant is just that, a constant, and will not change unless you use a different type of spring.
$PE = -GmM/r$ *(gravitational, general)*

40. C: From the question, doubling distance would lower the gravitational force by a factor of 1/4, since the force is proportional to $1/R^2$. The gravitational potential would be 1/2 of the original because it is proportional to 1/R. Therefore, the ratio of the new force to the new potential would be $1/4 \div 1/2$, or 1/2 of the original ratio.

41. B: The total energy of an isolated system is always conserved. However the mechanical energy may not be, since some mechanical energy could be converted into radiation (light) or heat (through friction). According to Einstein's famous equation $E = mc^2$, energy is (occasionally, like in nuclear reactions!) converted into mass, and vice versa, where c is the speed of light. This does not affect the conservation of energy law, however, since the mass is considered to have an energy equivalent. This equation does not tell anything about the mechanical energy of a particle; it just shows how much energy would be generated if the mass was converted directly into energy.

42. D: Answers A, B, and C all shed light on what conservative forces are but do not answer the question of why the work on an object doesn't depend on its path. Friction is a force that causes kinetic energy to be lost and where the amount of loss depends on the path taken. Work can be expressed in multiple ways, including as the sum of potentials, and all that matters is the beginning and ending position. Think of this in terms of gravity, gravitational potential energy, and the work done by gravity. In this case, $W = \Delta PE = mg\Delta h$, where h is an objects height. Dividing work by the change in position shows $mg = \Delta PE/\Delta h$. Since mg is a force, you can say $F = \Delta PE/\Delta h$, or the force equals the work/change in potential energy divided by its change in position.

43. B: Power is the amount of work done divided by the time it took to do the work. A kilowatt-hour is a unit of work. A 5 KW engine running for 12 hours produces 5 x 12 = 60 kilowatt-hours of work. At $0.06 per Kw-h, this is 60 x 0.06 = $3.60. The other answers all occur from simple math mistakes.

44. B: The wavelength is the distance (often in meters) between two peaks or two troughs of a wave. In this case, that distance is labeled as 4 meters. The height of the wave from the center is the amplitude. This wave has an amplitude of 5 meters, which is half of the total vertical distance from the top of one peak to the bottom of a trough. 2 meters represents 1/2 of the wavelength, which would be the horizontal distance across a single peak or trough, but not from peak to peak.

45. D: The phase of a wave changes as the wave moves. When measured in radians, the phase fluctuates between 0 and 2π radians. It is this fluctuating angle that allows two identical waves to be either in or out of phase, depending on whether their sinusoidal forms are matching or not when they cross. Answers A and B are meant to emulate the wave's amplitude and wavelength, both of which are measured in units of distance (meters, for example) and not radians.

46. D: The jumper's weight is 9.8 m/s^2 x 100 kg= 980 Newtons. Insert the weight—a force—into the equation F = kx, where k is the spring constant and x is the displacement from rest of the spring. The displacement here is 5 meters. 20 meters is unnecessary information, and just a measure of how long the spring is, not how far it was displaced. k = F/x = 980 N / 5 meters = 196 N/m.

47. C: The phase will cycle through 2π radians. Therefore, $(5.0 \text{ Hz})t = 2\pi$ and $t = 2\pi/5 = 1.26$ seconds.

Copyright © Mometrix Media. You have been licensed one copy of this document for personal use only. Any other reproduction or redistribution is strictly prohibited. All rights reserved.

48. C: Although the acceleration of a falling object is constant (9.8 m/s^2), this is not true for a pendulum. The total force on a simple pendulum is the resultant of the force of gravity on the bob acting downward and the tension in the string. When the pendulum is at the bottom of its swing, the net force is zero (tension = weight), although the bob does have a velocity. At the top of its swing, when it's changing direction, the tension is least. Therefore, the net force is greatest here, too. The bob is stationary momentarily at its highest level. Since F = ma, a large force means that the acceleration here is highest, too.

49. A: The Doppler effect shows that light/radiation from a object moving away has a longer wavelength. A car moving towards the RADAR gun would have a shorter wavelength. Since c = vf (where c = speed of light, v = wavelength and f = frequency), increasing the wavelength would cause the frequency to become smaller.

50. B: The speed of a wave is the product of its wavelength and frequency. V = vf. Here, $v = 12 \times 3 = 36 \text{ m/s}$.

51. A: The amplitude of waves that cross/interfere is the sum of the instantaneous height at the point the two waves cross. In this case, one wave is at its peak amplitude A. The other wave, in a trough, is at its minimum amplitude -A. Since these waves are at opposite heights, their sum = A + -A = 0. Had the waves both been peaking, the sum would be A + A = 2A. If they had both been at a minimum, the sum would be -2A.

52. C: As the amplitude of the pendulum increases due to resonance, it will swing higher. However, the period of a pendulum is not connected to how high it swings. Only the length of the pendulum affects its period. Obviously, the length of a pendulum will not be affected by how high it's swinging or whether it's in resonance.

53. A: A standing wave remains stationary, and the fixed points at both ends are the wave's nodes. Nevertheless, a standing waves with nodes at both ends of the string can have several forms. It may have one anti-node (i.e., it will arc across), two anti-nodes (this looks like a sine wave), three anti-nodes (with 1.5 sine waves), etc. However, waves with just one anti-node will the longest wavelength and thus the smallest frequency. For a wave with one anti-node, the string will have only ONE-HALF of a wave, so 20 m represents a half-wavelength and the full wavelength is 40 m. Using the wave equation ($v = \lambda f$) gives the correct answer. $f = v/\lambda = 4 \text{ m/s} / 40 \text{ m} = 0.1 \text{ Hz}$.

54. C: If the waves are 500 Hz and 504 Hz, they will have 504 - 500 = 4 beats per second. By definition, this would have a frequency of 4 Hz. This would mean 0.25 seconds between beats.

55. A: Refraction occurs when a wave enters a new medium. The boundary between the old medium and the new medium produces a reflected wave and a refracted wave. Since the medium is different, the speed and direction of the refracted wave changes. This changes the wavelength, but the frequency remains the same. The angle of reflection depends on the angle of incidence of the wave that strikes the boundary. The angle of refraction depends partly on this angle of incidence, but also on the indices of refraction of the two substances. Although refraction is defined as a wave changing direction when it enters a new substance, a wave will not change direction if it enters this new medium exactly perpendicular to the surface.

56. B: When a tuning fork vibrates it creates areas of condensation (higher pressure) and rarefactions (lower pressure) that propagate through the air because of the air's elasticity. The

Copyright © Mometrix Media. You have been licensed one copy of this document for personal use only. Any other reproduction or redistribution is strictly prohibited. All rights reserved.

distance between the condensations or rarefactions is the wavelength of the sound. The amplitude of the sound is half the difference between the pressure of the condensation and the pressure of the rarefaction. Loudness and power are both logarithmic measures that depend on the amplitude, but are not directly proportional to it. For example, doubling the amplitude will not double the loudness or power; those quantities will increase just slightly.

57. A: Sound travels much faster through helium than through air. Generally, the speed of sound can be calculated by speed = $\sqrt{(k \times P / \rho)}$, where k is the index of specific heats, P is pressure and ρ is density. Since helium has a much lower density, it would have a higher speed.

58. A: The frequency of a sound wave directly determines its pitch. We say the pitch of 480 Hz is higher than the pitch of 440 Hz. High and low are the words we use to describe pitch. Overtones refer to the frequencies above the fundamental frequency in a musical instrument. Two singers singing the same note at the same loudness will sound differently because their voices have different timbres.

59. C: Three full waves fit into the pipe, according to the question description. The wavelength of the third harmonic in this pipe organ is 1.2m/1.5 waves = 0.8 m. Using the wave equation ($v = \lambda f$), f = 340 m/s / 0.8 m = 425 Hz.

60. A: For standing waves, the string must be fixed at both ends. The wavelength at the fundamental frequency is 4 meters and the wavelength when the string resonates at the fourth harmonic is 1 meter. Using the wave equation $v = \lambda f$, the frequency at the fourth harmonic is v/1 m = 50 Hz. Hence the necessary speed is 50 m/s. Furthermore, the mass per unit length is 0.01 kg / 2 meters = 0.005 kg/m. Thus the tension is the string is $v^2 \times \mu = 50^2$ x 0.005 = 12.5 newtons.

61. B: Medical ultrasound machines use echolocation, in which sound waves are bounced off objects and the returning sound waves are used to create an image. This same process is also used by some animals, such as bats and dolphins. The spectrum of sound has three areas: infrasonic, audible, and ultrasonic. Humans can hear sound waves between 20 Hz and 20,000 Hz, so these are the cut-off points. The Doppler effect refers to the changing pitch of sound for objects that are moving towards or away from you.

62. B: The density of a homogeneous object, liquid, or gas is its mass divided by its volume or the ratio of its mass to its volume. Density is inversely proportional to the volume and directly proportional to the mass. The ratio of the density of A to the density of B is 5:4 or 5/4. Hence, the ratio of the volume of A to the volume of B is 4:5 or 4/5. Alternatively one could solve the equation $5V_A = 4V_B$.

63. C: If the sub stays at a constant depth, its buoyant force must be equal to its weight. If the buoyant force was larger, it would rise. If lower, it would sink. All objects underwater experience a buoyant force, so it cannot be zero.

64. A: Pascal's law is that the pressure on the input piston is equal to the pressure on the output piston. (To move the truck, of course, the input piston moves a much greater distance than the output piston.) Since the pressure depends on the area of the pistons, and the area = πr^2, you need only find the ratio of the two areas to find the necessary force. Since the diameter is twice the radius, you can simplify this step by taking the ratio of the square of the diameters. $2^2 / 24^2$ = 0.007. Multiplying this by the weight of the car gets 0.007 x 3500 N = 24 N. Remember also that the point of a hydraulic lift is to reduce the force, not increase it.

Copyright © Mometrix Media. You have been licensed one copy of this document for personal use only. Any other reproduction or redistribution is strictly prohibited. All rights reserved.

65. C: The pressure of water at a depth h is given by ρgh where ρ is the density of water. Here P = (1000 kg/m³ x 9.8 m/s² x 14 m) = 1.37 x 10⁵ N/m². To find the force of the water on the window, multiply this pressure by the window's area. F = π(1m)² x 1.37 x 10⁵ N/m² = 4.3 x 10⁵ N/m².

66. B: To increase the flow rate, you'd want to: (1) reduce the length L of the pipe, (2) make the pipe wider, and (3) have a fluid with low viscosity (just think of how much slower a viscous fluid like molasses runs as compared to water). Answer B is the only answer that describes all of these changes.

67. C: In an ideal fluid, from the conservation of mass, ρvA is constant. Since the area (A) decreases by a factor 3²/5² = 0.36, the speed increases by 5²/3². So 6 m/s x 5²/3² = 16.7 m/s. Incompressible means the density (ρ) is a constant. An ideal fluid has no viscosity, there is no rotational flow, and the flow is the same throughout the liquid, so answer D is not correct.
Concept of turbulence at high velocities

68. D: Irrotational fluid flow consists of streamlines which describe the paths taken by the fluid elements. The streamlines don't have to be straight lines because the pipe may be curved. Answer B describes the conditions for steady flow. The image of a paddle wheel may be used to explain irrotational flow, but (1) the wheel will not turn in an irrotational fluid flow, and (2) this only works if the viscosity is zero. When there is viscosity, the speed of the fluid near the surface of the pipe is less than the speed of the fluid in the center of a pipe. Rotational flow includes vortex motion, whirlpools, and eddies.

69. C: In a vacuum the only forces acting on the molecules of aluminum are other aluminum molecules. Inside a fluid, the molecules of the fluid collide with the sides of cube and exert a force on the surface causing the cube to shrink in size slightly. Also, the temperature of water deep in the ocean is very low. This causes the vibratory motion of the aluminum molecules to decrease, which decreases the dimensions of the cube.

70. A: When an external force deforms a solid material, it will return to its initial position when the force is removed. This is called elasticity and is exhibited by springs. If too much force is applied and the elastic limit is exceeded, the rod won't return to its original shape any longer. As with springs, the deformation is directly proportional to the stress. The elastic limit occurs in rods subjected to a tensile force when the strain stops being directly proportional to the stress. The typical pattern when the force increases is that the strain increases linearly, then it doesn't increase as much, and then it breaks.

71. B: As water freezes and becomes a solid, that heat leaves the water and the temperature of the water decreases. Water is a rare exception to the rule because it expands when it freezes. Most other substances contract when they freeze because the average distance between the atoms of the substance decreases. Water, on the other hand, forms a crystal lattice when it freezes, which causes the Hydrogen and Oxygen molecules to move slightly further away from each other due to the lattice's rigid structure. The coefficient of thermal expansion is always positive. Answer C just restates the phenomena and does not give an explanation. Answer D is true but does not explain the expansion of freezing water.

72. D: The bulk modulus describes a substance's reaction to being squeezed and its change in volume, which directly affects its density. The elastic modulus is the ratio of stress to strain for an

Copyright © Mometrix Media. You have been licensed one copy of this document for personal use only. Any other reproduction or redistribution is strictly prohibited. All rights reserved.

object. Young's modulus deals with the elasticity and length of an object. The shear modulus deals with the elasticity of a shape and the stress that's applied perpendicular to its surfaces.

73. B: If the charged object is negative, it will cause electrons in the neutral object to move away from the charged object. If the charged object is positive, it will attract electrons. In both cases, there will be an attractive force. There is also an induced repulsive force, but the repulsive force is less because the like charges are farther away. An object has a net charge because electrons have been added to a neutral object or electrons have been removed from the atoms, ions, or molecules in the object.

74. B: Although Answer A is also true, Answer B correctly states the law of conservation of charge. Answer C is only partially true because there are other elementary particles with a charge. Answer D is false because a photon will produce an electron-positron pair. There is also the example of a proton and electron combining to form a neutron.

75. B: Answer B correctly states the definition of a conductor. Answer C is incorrect because a current will also flow in an insulator, for example, although that current will be very low. In metals, the current flow caused by an electric field is much greater than in an insulator or semiconductor because the electrons are not bound to any particular atom, but are free to move. Answer D is incorrect because a vacuum tube is a device that electrons can flow in, but a vacuum tube is not considered a conductor.

76. D: The third charge, which is positive, will be repelled by the charge of $+2q$ and attracted to the charge of $-q$. For this reason, the third charge can't be between the two other charges and have a net force of 0, since it would always jointly be pushed and pulled towards the negative charge. It must be past the more distant negative charge. If the charge were situated at a distance of $2d$ from the origin, which is distance d from the negative charge, it would have a repulsive force of $F = k (q)(2q) / (2d)^2$ and an attractive force of $F = k (q)(q) / (d)^2$, meaning the attractive force is still too small by $1/2$ the repulsive force. Thus the particle must be past the distance of $2d$, or Answer D. If you solve this distance quadratically, the particle is at $3.41 d$.

77. C: The electric field at a point in space is the force acting on a small positive test charge divided by the magnitude of the test charge. Its units are newtons per coulomb and it is a vector pointing in the direction of the force. The electric field produced by a charge distribution refers to the electric fields at each point in space. All the electric field vectors are tangent to electric field lines or electric lines of force. The electric field produced by a charge distribution can be represented by all the electric field vectors. Or, it can be represented by electric field lines. In this case, the stronger the electric field the closer together the electric field lines are. Arrows on the lines indicate the direction of the electric field. Answer D is incorrect because the field is being represented by electric field lines, not electric field vectors.

78. B: Concerning answer A, if an object has a positive charge, it is because electrons were removed. In the case of a conductor, the electrons will migrate away from the surface, leaving a positive charge on the surface. The electric field of a negative point charge points towards the charge. The electric field of a sheet of charges will be perpendicular to the sheet.

79. B: The direction of the electric field is the same as the direction of the force on a positive test charge. Moving a negative charge in the direction of the electric field requires an external force to oppose the electric field. This would increase the electron's potential energy.

Copyright © Mometrix Media. You have been licensed one copy of this document for personal use only. Any other reproduction or redistribution is strictly prohibited. All rights reserved.

80. D: Dipoles -- meaning two poles -- are either electric or magnetic, but represent a simple a pair of opposite charges with equal magnitude. Just as a magnet cannot have only one pole, many physicists believe it's impossible to have a mono-pole, which has only one pole. Dipoles are important in chemistry because many molecules, water for example, are polarized. The charges in nonpolar molecules are uniformly distributed throughout the molecule. The oxygen side of a water molecule has a net negative charge and the hydrogen side has a net positive charge because the charges are not uniformly distributed.

81. A: Since like charges repel and opposite charges attract, putting a dipole in an electric field would cause the dipole to orient so that its negative side will point towards the electric field's positive side. Since electric fields flow from positive towards negative, an electric field pointing from south to north could be caused by positive charges in the south and negative charges in the north. Consequently, the dipole will line up opposite to this, with the positive charge on the north side. Answer B is not correct because such an orientation would be unstable. The least disturbance would cause the dipole to flip 180°.

82. B: The electric potential, which comes from the electrostatic potential energy, is the potential of a charged particle in an electrical field. The stronger the field or the higher the charge, the higher the potential. So putting a point charge near a dipole will create a potential, depending on how strong the dipole's field is. For a potential of 0, you would need to be far from the dipole, so its electric field strength was effectively 0. At an infinite distance from a dipole, the distance between the charges is approximately 0 meters, so the net charge is 0 coulombs.

83. C: This is a classroom demonstration of electrostatics. The paper is initially charged by induction and is attracted to the comb. When in contact with the comb, electrons migrate from the paper to the comb and the paper acquires a positive charge. Answer B might be true, but the transfer of electrons from the paper to the comb occurs before the transfer of electrons from the air to the comb.

84. B: This is Gauss's law, which concerns electric field lines. Electric field lines leave positive charges and enter negative charges. Electric field lines entering a surface are positive and electric field lines leaving a surface are negative. If there is no charge inside the surface, the sum of the electric field lines is zero. Coulomb's law refers to attractive force between any two charged particles. Faraday's law regards the creation of electric fields from moving magnetic fields. The Biot-Savart law concerns the creation of magnetic fields from moving charges.

85. C: The force $F = qvB \sin\theta = (1.6 \times 10^{-19}$ coulombs$)(8.0 \times 10^6$ m/s$)(0.5$ T$) \sin(45) = 4.5 \times 10^{-13}$ N.

86. B: For a positively charged particle, you would used the right hand rule (RHR) to solve this. Since this is an electron, you can either use the left hand rule, or use the RHR and switch the direction of the inducted force. The RHR gives you the direction of a force exerted by a magnetic field on a magnetic field. When holding your right hand flat, the fingers point in the direction of the velocity of a positive charge, the palm points in the direction of the magnetic field, and the thumb points in the direction of the magnetic force. For a negative charge, the force is in the opposite direction, or downward in this case.

87. B: A moving electron produces a circular magnetic field that is perpendicular to the velocity of the particle. Since the magnetic field produced by the electron exerts a magnetic force towards the electron, the charge on the particle is positive. This conclusion requires the correct application of the right-hand rule for the creation of a magnetic field by a current (thumb in the direction of the

Copyright © Mometrix Media. You have been licensed one copy of this document for personal use only. Any other reproduction or redistribution is strictly prohibited. All rights reserved.

velocity of a positive charge with fingers curling in the direction of the magnetic field) and the right-hand rule for the magnetic force on a moving charge (fingers in the direction of the positively charged particle's velocity, thumb in the direction of the magnetic force, and palm in the direction of the magnetic field). Answer D is wrong because there are no particles with only a north pole or a south pole. There may be a force between the electron and the particle if the particle is a tiny magnet, but the direction of the force would depend on the magnet's orientation, and hence answer A is wrong.

88. A: Solenoids create a magnetic field inside the coils. Outside the solenoid, the magnetic field is practically zero, so increasing the number of coils won't have much effect on the exterior field strength. Inside the coils, increasing the number and density of coils increases the field strength.

89. C: In a vacuum, the speed of light has nothing to do with its wavelength, frequency or color. It's a constant 3×10^8 m/s. When light travels through a medium other than a vacuum, such as glass or a prism, it slows down, and technically different colors of light travel at slightly different speeds. However, in most physics problems, you should treat all light as traveling at the same speed.

90. B: Although the wavelength of light is related to its color, the frequency really determines light's color. For example, light slows down when it enters water. This doesn't change the frequency or the color of light, but it does change its wavelength. The fact that light sometimes acts like a wave and sometimes acts like particles is called "duality." The energy of light can be expressed as $E = h\nu$, where h is the Plank's constant and ν is the frequency.

91. C: Radio waves have the lowest frequency and the longest wavelength. Microwaves also have low frequencies and long wavelengths compared to visible light. X-rays are highly energetic and have higher frequencies and smaller wavelengths than visible light.

92. D: "Conventional current" -- as is typically used in physics and elsewhere -- is the flow of positive charges from the positive to negative sides of a battery. In reality, protons don't actually move through a wire. Negatively charged electrons move, so conventional current really reflects the effective positive charge created by electrons moving in the opposite direction. Normally, the wide side of the battery represents the positive side, so conventional current would start from the wide side and move around until it reached the narrow side of the battery. Here, the batteries aren't labeled with positive or negative. However, that doesn't matter, since the batteries are oriented in opposite directions. If they had the same exact voltage, no current would flow. However, if one battery has a higher voltage than the other, the higher voltage battery would dominate the direction of current flow. Since you don't know the voltage of the batteries, you cannot determine the direction of current flow.

93. D: Current can be expressed as the flow of charge per time, which Answers A and C both express. Answer B follows from the units in Ohm's law, V = IR. Answer D is the only incorrect way of expressing current, although watts per volts would be an OK way to express amperes, which follows from the Power equation P = IV.

94. A: In a Zn-Cu battery, the zinc terminal has a higher concentration of electrons than the copper terminal, so there is a potential difference between the locations of the two terminals. This is a form of electrical energy brought about by the chemical interactions between the metals and the electrolyte the battery uses. Creating a circuit and causing a current to flow will transform the electrical energy into heat energy, mechanical energy, or another form of electrical energy,

Copyright © Mometrix Media. You have been licensed one copy of this document for personal use only. Any other reproduction or redistribution is strictly prohibited. All rights reserved.

depending on the devices in the circuit. A generator transforms mechanical energy into electrical energy and a transformer changes the electrical properties of a form of electrical energy.

95. C: Ohm's law is that $V = IR$. Answer C is the only relation that holds true using this equation. If the resistance doesn't change, increasing the current on the right side must cause the voltage to also increase on the left side.

96. B: Since the ammeter is connected in series, it will draw current and reduce the current in the resistor. However, ammeters have a very small resistance so as to draw as little current as possible. That way, measuring the current doesn't significantly affect the amount of current traveling through a circuit. Voltmeters, on the other hand, are connected in parallel and have a high resistance.

97. B: For resistors in series, the total resistance is the sum of their individual resistances. For resistors in parallel, the total resistance is given by $1/R = 1/R_1 + 1/R_2 + \ldots$ First, the bottom two resistors have a total resistance of 2 Ω+ 4 Ω= 6 Ω. Then add this in parallel with the 3 Ohm resistor. $1/R = 1/3 + 1/6 = 1/2$. So R = 2 Ω for the bottom three elements. To find the total resistance, add this in series to the top resistor, for a total R = 10 Ω + 2Ω = 12Ω.

98. A: Answer A would be correct if the temperature of the two wires was the same. Wires have the least resistance when they are short and fat. This is expressed as R = ρL / A, where ρ is the resistivity of the substance, L is the length and A is the area. Since both wires are tungsten, they must have the same resistivity. So doubling the length and area adds a factor of 2 to both the top and bottom of the equation, giving no change in overall resistance.

99. C: A capacitor connected to a battery with a small internal resistance will charge up very quickly because of the high current flow. Once the potential difference on the two plates becomes equal to the emf of the battery, the electrons will stop flowing from the positive plate to the negative plate and the capacitor will be fully charged up. Connecting the capacitor to a battery with a greater emf will cause the plates to acquire a greater charge. However, the charge is directly proportional to the voltage. The capacitance is the ratio of charge to voltage and depends only on the physical characteristics of the capacitor.

100. B: Answers A and C are wrong because they doesn't have the units of energy (joules). To make things easier, the correct answer follows the same form as other kinds of energy (KE = ½mv2, a spring's potential energy is ½kx^2, etc.) The capacitance is defined as Q/V, so the energy is proportional to QV. The potential at a point in space is determined by the concentration of charge at that point, but the potential difference (V = work/charge) is defined in terms of the motion of a small test charge. At the very beginning of the process of charging up a capacitor, the work needed to move a test charge from the positive plate to the negative plate is 0 volts. As the capacitor charges up, more energy is required to move the charge because the charge is repelled by the negative plate. The total energy stored is Q × average voltage. Since the voltage increases linearly, the average voltage is ½ V.

101. A: Since these capacitors are connected in series you must add the reciprocals of their capacitance. $1/C_{total} = 1/C_1 + 1/C_2$. So $1/C_{total} = 1/3 + 1/6 = 1/2$. Thus C_{total} =2 microfarads.

102. C: When capacitors are connected in parallel the voltage drop across each capacitor is equal to the electromotive force of the battery ($V = V_1 = V_2$). Because these capacitors are in parallel, you can simply add their capacitances to find the total capacitance.

Copyright © Mometrix Media. You have been licensed one copy of this document for personal use only. Any other reproduction or redistribution is strictly prohibited. All rights reserved.

103. A: The current that flows in the resistor connected to the battery without the capacitor is 5×10^{-5} ampere. When the battery is disconnected this is the initial current as the electrons flow from the negative plate through the resistor to the positive plate. As electrons build up on the positive plate, the current decreases. The decrease is exponential, so the capacitor never fully loses its charge. Answer B is the time constant for the RC circuit (resistance × capacitance). After 30 seconds, the current is 37% of its initial value. When the time lapsed is three times RC, the current will be reduced to 95%. Within a short time, the current will be so small it will not be measureable with an ammeter, although it will technically never fully discharge.

104. B: Power is the rate at which work is done. It can be expressed as $P = VI$ or $P = IR^2$. With 10 volts and 50 watts, the current is $I = P/V = 50w / 10v = 5$ amps. Current is measured in coulombs/second, watts in joules/second, and volts in joules/coulomb. Answer D is equivalent to 5 amps since the charge on an electron is 1.6×10^{-19} coulombs.

105. A: The maximum current is derived from Ohm's law. $I = V / R = 40\ V / 20\ ohms = 2$ amps. However, because this is an alternating current, the instantaneous current actually fluctuates between +2 amps and -2 amps. Electrons effectively move back and forth. This means the average current is 0 amps.

106. D: For constructive interference, the waves must arrive having the same phase. Therefore, neither answers A nor B can be correct. Constructive interference occurs when the waveforms add together, producing a maximum that is twice as intense as either of the individual waves. Answer C would cause the waves to be out of phase by 1, 3, 5 or 7 (etc.) half-wavelengths, meaning the waves would be out of phase by a half-wavelength. Only Answer D assures that the two waves arrive in phase.

107. B: The two slits cause the light beams to diffract, that is, spread out instead of travelling in a straight line. As a result there are two light beams superimposed on one another. When the two light beams constructively interfere there are bright lines, and when the two light beams destructively interfere there are dark lines. Chromatic aberration has to do blurring through a lens due to different colors of light. Doppler shift affects the wavelength of light from moving sources. Total internal reflection is 100% reflection of light at the boundary between certain materials.

108. A: Diffraction gratings produce so much destructive interference that large distances separate the bright lines due to interference. This means diffraction gratings can be used to separate light consisting of different wave lengths. Answer B is wrong because blue light, which has a shorter wavelength than red light, refracts and diffracts less than red light. The greater the wavelength of light, the more it changes direction when it hits an edge.

109. A: Polarization is a property of transverse waves when the medium vibrates in the direction perpendicular to the direction of propagation of energy. A polarizer orients these waves so they're all oscillating in the same direction. Polarization is a property of waves, not particles, so the particle nature of light cannot be used to polarize light. Nor are there tiny holes in a polarizer, although there are thin lines. The fact that light travels in a vacuum means that light does not need a medium, but does not affect polarization. Also, light travels in transverse, not longitudinal waves.

110. C: The emission of light is caused by photons of a specific frequency striking gas molecules, which excites their electrons and eventually causes them to emit light. Since this light comes in very specific colors, it implies that light comes is specific quanta. The ultraviolet catastrophe refers to the

Copyright © Mometrix Media. You have been licensed one copy of this document for personal use only. Any other reproduction or redistribution is strictly prohibited. All rights reserved.

frequency distribution of light emitted by a blackbody. A black body is, basically, a hot object that emits radiation in a predictable pattern. The threshold frequency refers to the photoelectric effect. The stability of atoms is a quantum phenomena, however it is only indirectly connected to the existence of light quanta.

111. B: Laser is an acronym from *light amplification by stimulated emission of radiation.* Lasers produce light because the substance used goes into a relatively stable excited state before emitting light. In phosphorescence, a substance absorbs light and goes into a relatively stable excited state. Light is re-emitted at a later point in time. Radioactivity produces different types of radiation from unstable nuclei. Sunlight comes from nuclear reactions on the sun. Blackbody radiation comes from hot materials and not from the transition of atoms from a higher energy state to a lower energy state.

112. B: Specular reflection occurs with smooth surfaces such as mirrors or a water puddle. All of the light is not necessarily reflected because there can be refraction and absorption. Answer A is wrong because a rough surface consists of many smooth surfaces oriented in different directions, so the light will not necessarily reflect at the same angle as incidence. Note, however, that for each small surface on a rough tabletop, for example, the angle of incidence is equal to the angle of reflection.

113. C: The angles of incidence and refraction are defined as the angle made by the rays with a line perpendicular to the surface. The angles of incidence and refraction are given by Snell's law: $n_1 \sin \theta_1 = n_2 \sin \theta_2$. In this case, because glass has a higher index of refraction (n) than air, the angle of refraction will be smaller than the angle of incidence. Increasing the angle of incidence by 5 degrees will increase the angle of refraction, but it will still be below the original 45°. Proving this with Snell's law: 1.0 x sin (50) = 1.3 sin(θ), so Sin(θ) = 0.59 and θ = 36°.

114. C: A ray of sunlight consists of many different colors of light. The speed of red light in water is slightly larger than the speed of violet light, so the angle of refraction of violet light is greater than that of red light. This causes the light to separate and creates a spectrum of colors, like in a prism. Raindrops do exhibit total internal reflection for all the wavelengths inside the droplet, although this is not what causes the rainbow. Instead, this causes a second refraction as the sunlight emerges from the water droplet, which can sometimes been seen in nature as a "double rainbow."

115. C: Snell's law is $n_1 \sin \theta_1 = n_2 \sin \theta_2$. This means the angle of refraction is greater than or less than the angle of incidence depending on which index of refraction is bigger. It also gives the critical angle at which there is no refracted beam. This only happens when light is in a substance with a high index of refraction and strikes a substance with a lower angle of refraction at a large angle of incidence. That light slows down when leaving a vacuum coupled with the wave nature of light leads to Snell's law. It is not relevant to understanding total internal reflection that light consists of quanta and is transverse electric and magnetic fields.

116. D: Parallel rays striking a concave mirror intersect at the focal point. If the rays weren't parallel — say they were both coming from an object near the mirror — then they would intersect elsewhere, depending on the focal length and their distance from the mirror. For example, Answer B would be correct if the rays both started at the focal point. For an object between the focal point and the mirror, the virtual image is created by extending the rays geometrically behind the mirror. The center of curvature is at the center of the sphere that defines the spherical mirror and is equal to twice the focal length.

Copyright © Mometrix Media. You have been licensed one copy of this document for personal use only. Any other reproduction or redistribution is strictly prohibited. All rights reserved.

117. C: Convex is the opposite of concave. A convex mirror bulges outward like the outside of a sphere. They always produce a small image that is right side up. These images are always virtual, also, meaning the image appears to lie behind the mirror. A convex mirror with an infinite radius of curvature is essentially a plane mirror.

118. C: A magnifying glass is a convex lens, just like the lens used in a telescope or microscope. For objects located beyond the focal point of the lens, the image is inverted (upside down) and real. For objects located between the focal point and the lens, the image is virtual and erect (right side up). The focal length is determined by the radii of curvature of the two lens surfaces and the index of refraction of the lens material.

119. D: Since the lens is convex, the focal length is positive and the image will appear behind the lens. You can use the lens equation to solve this. $1/f = 1/o + 1/i$, where f is the coal length, i is the image location and o is the object location. Since the object is in front it has a positive sign. $1/10$ cm $= 1/20$ cm $+ 1/i$, so $1/i = 1/20$ and $i = 20$ cm. The positive sign for the image means that it is behind the lens.

120. A: The magnification of a lens can be calculated from its image distance, i, and its object distance, o. $M = i/o$. Here $M = 19/49 = 0.39$.

121. C: Adding a second concave lens will shorten the focal length, thereby eliminating answers A and B. To find this total, you need to add their reciprocals: $1/f = 1/30 + 1/30 = 2/30$. So $f = 30/2 = 15$ cm. You would follow this same procedure if the second lens had been concave, except the focal length would then have been a negative number.

122. B: This question is asking about a concave MIRROR, not a lens. Since light does not pass through a mirror—it only reflects off of it—the different colors of light all bend the same amount. If light was passing through a lens, the different colors would bend slightly different amounts, causing chromatic aberration. That's not the case here. Spherical aberration occurs because the focal point of the mirror changes slightly as you move away from the center (optical axis). Astigmatism occurs when incident rays are not parallel to the optical axis. A circular beam, striking a lens or mirror at an angle to the optical axis, will become a parabola. Distortion concerns magnification and occurs in both mirrors and lenses.

123. D: All of these principles are true except Snell's Law. Snell's law is $1.0 \times \sin(\theta_{incident}) = n \times \sin(\theta_{refraction})$ for a ray striking a transparent substance from a vacuum. It is true for all rays striking a lens. However, this is not a principle used in ray diagrams. Although light is bent when it enters the lens, as Snell's Law describes, it returns to its original direction when it leaves the lens. To simplify this process, it's often best to assume that a lens is infinitely thin when solving many physics problems.

124. C: To find the total magnification, multiply the magnification of the three lenses. The magnification of a lens is the ratio of the object size to the image size and is the negative of the ratio of the object distance to the image distance. The sign is positive if the image is upright and negative if the image is inverted. Answer A comes from adding the magnifications instead of multiplying the magnifications. Answer D has the wrong the sign.

125. A: When electrons drop to the ground level, they emit energy. In the same way, they can absorb energy and jump from the ground state to an excited state, or from an excited state to a more excited state. To completely ionize a Hydrogen atom — for an electron to jump from the

Copyright © Mometrix Media. You have been licensed one copy of this document for personal use only. Any other reproduction or redistribution is strictly prohibited. All rights reserved.

ground level and completely escape—takes 13.2 eV. However, it takes less energy to simply jump from the ground level to the first excited state. However, most of the energy needed to escape is used for that first jump. Answer C would be correct if the transition was from $n = 3$ to n = 2. Answer B would be correct if the hydrogen atom in the ground state was ionized by the absorption of a photon. Answer D would be correct if the hydrogen atom absorbed a photon and became more excited.

126. C: In 2.4×10^4 years, 50% of the substance will have decayed. In another half-life, half of this will be gone, or 75%. 87.5% represents 3 half lives, or a total of 3 x 2.4×10^4 years = 7.2×10^4 years.

127. B: Fission means the nucleus breaks up into two smaller nuclei. When certain nuclear isotopes absorb a neutron, they become unstable and split, starting the process of fission. The average binding energy per nucleon increases with a fission reaction, and the two new nuclei are more stable than the initial nucleus. The increase in binding energy comes from the mass of the protons and neutrons (note: both protons and neutrons are nucleons). The release of energy is part of the fission reaction and does not explain why the fission reaction occurs.

128. C: Sunlight consists of photons and cosmic rays. Sunlight is produces when hydrogen, deuterium, and tritium nuclei combine to form helium. This nuclear reaction is called fusion. Fission occurs when a nucleus disintegrates into two smaller nuclei. In both fission and fusion, energy is released because the binding energy per nucleon increases. This decreases the mass of the nuclei.

129. A: In a nuclear reaction, be it fission or fusion, matter is converted into energy. Einstein first postulated the law of energy-mass conservation using the equation $E = mc^2$, where m is mass, E is energy and c is the speed of light. Looking closely at this equation shows that a tiny amount of matter can produce a large amount of energy, which is why nuclear reactions are so energetic.

130. C: Protons and neutrons are both considered nucleons. The number of nucleons in a nucleus is called the *mass number*. Isotopes of the same element have different mass numbers. But since they are the same element, they must have the same atomic number, which is equal to the number of protons. Thus, only the number of neutrons changes, since electron's mass is so low that it doesn't have much effect on the mass number of an element. Unless they are also ionized, they would have the same number of protons and electrons.

131. C: An alpha particle is two protons bound together with two neutrons. Since it doesn't have any electrons, it has a charge of +2. Emitting an alpha particle causes the atomic number of the nucleus to decrease by two, and its mass to decrease by approximately four atomic mass units. Exactly how much the mass decreases depends on the binding energies of the two nuclei. Its charge decreases by two.

132. A: Cobalt-63 has too many neutrons to be stable. By emitting a beta particle (aka an electron) one of the neutrons in the cobalt is converted to a proton, thereby maintaining the mass number but changing the atomic number from 27 (cobalt) to 28 (nickel). In addition, some energy is radiated away in the form of gamma particles. Electron emission is usually associated with the emission of gamma rays because the daughter nucleus is not likely to be in a ground state. The daughter nucleus, in other words, is likely to be unstable and emit a gamma ray.

133. A: An inch is about 2.54 cm = 25.4 mm = 2.54×10^{-5} km = 2.54×10^{-2} m.

Copyright © Mometrix Media. You have been licensed one copy of this document for personal use only. Any other reproduction or redistribution is strictly prohibited. All rights reserved.

134. D: There are only 2 significant digits in A. Answers B and C have 5 significant digits. Answer D has 6 significant digits.

135. C: In physics, systematic errors occur when comparing a theoretical value with an experimental value. The experimental value differed from the actual by 2.1 pounds, which is the systematic error. Since there is always random error, Answer A is incorrect. But random error is just that — random— so it cannot be 2.1 pound, which is systematic because it's a consistent error due to the method used to take this measurement.

136. D: Because you do not know the exact distribution of heights, Answer D is correct. The deviation of a measurement is the difference between the mean (average measurement) and the measurement. The standard deviation is the square root of the mean of the deviations squared. On average, about 68% of a sample will fall within one standard deviation. So if the standard deviation is 0.05 meters, ABOUT 68% of the students will stand between 1.64 +/- 0.05 meters. But this is only true if you have a fairly normal distribution of values. Similarly, this does not mean that half of the students are necessarily taller or shorter than the average. Since it is an average, you could have a class with a 20-foot giant and seven 5-foot-tall students and have an average that is a fairly large 6.857 feet. Answer C refers to the Mode, which looks for the most popular value.

Copyright © Mometrix Media. You have been licensed one copy of this document for personal use only. Any other reproduction or redistribution is strictly prohibited. All rights reserved.

Secret Key #1 - Time is Your Greatest Enemy

Pace Yourself

Wear a watch. At the beginning of the test, check the time (or start a chronometer on your watch to count the minutes), and check the time after every few questions to make sure you are "on schedule."

If you are forced to speed up, do it efficiently. Usually one or more answer choices can be eliminated without too much difficulty. Above all, don't panic. Don't speed up and just begin guessing at random choices. By pacing yourself, and continually monitoring your progress against your watch, you will always know exactly how far ahead or behind you are with your available time. If you find that you are one minute behind on the test, don't skip one question without spending any time on it, just to catch back up. Take 15 fewer seconds on the next four questions, and after four questions you'll have caught back up. Once you catch back up, you can continue working each problem at your normal pace.

Furthermore, don't dwell on the problems that you were rushed on. If a problem was taking up too much time and you made a hurried guess, it must be difficult. The difficult questions are the ones you are most likely to miss anyway, so it isn't a big loss. It is better to end with more time than you need than to run out of time.

Lastly, sometimes it is beneficial to slow down if you are constantly getting ahead of time. You are always more likely to catch a careless mistake by working more slowly than quickly, and among very high-scoring test takers (those who are likely to have lots of time left over), careless errors affect the score more than mastery of material.

Secret Key #2 - Guessing is not Guesswork

You probably know that guessing is a good idea - unlike other standardized tests, there is no penalty for getting a wrong answer. Even if you have no idea about a question, you still have a 20-25% chance of getting it right.

Most test takers do not understand the impact that proper guessing can have on their score. Unless you score extremely high, guessing will significantly contribute to your final score.

Monkeys Take the Test

What most test takers don't realize is that to insure that 20-25% chance, you have to guess randomly. If you put 20 monkeys in a room to take this test, assuming they answered once per question and behaved themselves, on average they would get 20-25% of the questions correct. Put 20 test takers in the room, and the average will be much lower among guessed questions. Why?

Copyright © Mometrix Media. You have been licensed one copy of this document for personal use only. Any other reproduction or redistribution is strictly prohibited. All rights reserved.

1. The test writers intentionally write deceptive answer choices that "look" right. A test taker has no idea about a question, so picks the "best looking" answer, which is often wrong. The monkey has no idea what looks good and what doesn't, so will consistently be lucky about 20-25% of the time.

2. Test takers will eliminate answer choices from the guessing pool based on a hunch or intuition. Simple but correct answers often get excluded, leaving a 0% chance of being correct. The monkey has no clue, and often gets lucky with the best choice.

This is why the process of elimination endorsed by most test courses is flawed and detrimental to your performance- test takers don't guess, they make an ignorant stab in the dark that is usually worse than random.

$5 Challenge

Let me introduce one of the most valuable ideas of this course- the $5 challenge:

You only mark your "best guess" if you are willing to bet $5 on it.
You only eliminate choices from guessing if you are willing to bet $5 on it.

Why $5? Five dollars is an amount of money that is small yet not insignificant, and can really add up fast (20 questions could cost you $100). Likewise, each answer choice on one question of the test will have a small impact on your overall score, but it can really add up to a lot of points in the end.

The process of elimination IS valuable. The following shows your chance of guessing it right:

If you eliminate wrong answer choices until only this many remain:	Chance of getting it correct:
1	100%
2	50%
3	33%

However, if you accidentally eliminate the right answer or go on a hunch for an incorrect answer, your chances drop dramatically: to 0%. By guessing among all the answer choices, you are GUARANTEED to have a shot at the right answer.

That's why the $5 test is so valuable- if you give up the advantage and safety of a pure guess, it had better be worth the risk.

What we still haven't covered is how to be sure that whatever guess you make is truly random. Here's the easiest way:

Always pick the first answer choice among those remaining.

Copyright © Mometrix Media. You have been licensed one copy of this document for personal use only. Any other reproduction or redistribution is strictly prohibited. All rights reserved.

Such a technique means that you have decided, **before you see a single test question**, exactly how you are going to guess- and since the order of choices tells you nothing about which one is correct, this guessing technique is perfectly random.

This section is not meant to scare you away from making educated guesses or eliminating choices- you just need to define when a choice is worth eliminating. The $5 test, along with a pre-defined random guessing strategy, is the best way to make sure you reap all of the benefits of guessing.

Secret Key #3 - Practice Smarter, Not Harder

Many test takers delay the test preparation process because they dread the awful amounts of practice time they think necessary to succeed on the test. We have refined an effective method that will take you only a fraction of the time.
There are a number of "obstacles" in your way to succeed. Among these are answering questions, finishing in time, and mastering test-taking strategies. All must be executed on the day of the test at peak performance, or your score will suffer. The test is a mental marathon that has a large impact on your future.

Just like a marathon runner, it is important to work your way up to the full challenge. So first you just worry about questions, and then time, and finally strategy:

Success Strategy

1. Find a good source for practice tests.
2. If you are willing to make a larger time investment, consider using more than one study guide- often the different approaches of multiple authors will help you "get" difficult concepts.
3. Take a practice test with no time constraints, with all study helps "open book." Take your time with questions and focus on applying strategies.
4. Take a practice test with time constraints, with all guides "open book."
5. Take a final practice test with no open material and time limits

If you have time to take more practice tests, just repeat step 5. By gradually exposing yourself to the full rigors of the test environment, you will condition your mind to the stress of test day and maximize your success.

Secret Key #4 - Prepare, Don't Procrastinate

Let me state an obvious fact: if you take the test three times, you will get three different scores. This is due to the way you feel on test day, the level of preparedness you have, and, despite the test writers' claims to the contrary, some tests WILL be easier for you than others.

Copyright © Mometrix Media. You have been licensed one copy of this document for personal use only. Any other reproduction or redistribution is strictly prohibited. All rights reserved.

Since your future depends so much on your score, you should maximize your chances of success. In order to maximize the likelihood of success, you've got to prepare in advance. This means taking practice tests and spending time learning the information and test taking strategies you will need to succeed.

Never take the test as a "practice" test, expecting that you can just take it again if you need to. Feel free to take sample tests on your own, but when you go to take the official test, be prepared, be focused, and do your best the first time!

Secret Key #5 - Test Yourself

Everyone knows that time is money. There is no need to spend too much of your time or too little of your time preparing for the test. You should only spend as much of your precious time preparing as is necessary for you to get the score you need.

Once you have taken a practice test under real conditions of time constraints, then you will know if you are ready for the test or not.
If you have scored extremely high the first time that you take the practice test, then there is not much point in spending countless hours studying. You are already there.

Benchmark your abilities by retaking practice tests and seeing how much you have improved. Once you score high enough to guarantee success, then you are ready.

If you have scored well below where you need, then knuckle down and begin studying in earnest. Check your improvement regularly through the use of practice tests under real conditions. Above all, don't worry, panic, or give up. The key is perseverance!

Then, when you go to take the test, remain confident and remember how well you did on the practice tests. If you can score high enough on a practice test, then you can do the same on the real thing.

General Strategies

The most important thing you can do is to ignore your fears and jump into the test immediately- do not be overwhelmed by any strange-sounding terms. You have to jump into the test like jumping into a pool- all at once is the easiest way.

Make Predictions

As you read and understand the question, try to guess what the answer will be. Remember that several of the answer choices are wrong, and once you begin reading them, your mind will immediately become cluttered with answer choices designed to throw you off. Your mind is typically the most focused immediately after you have read the question and digested its contents. If you can, try to predict what the correct answer will be. You may be surprised at what you can predict.

Copyright © Mometrix Media. You have been licensed one copy of this document for personal use only. Any other reproduction or redistribution is strictly prohibited. All rights reserved.

Quickly scan the choices and see if your prediction is in the listed answer choices. If it is, then you can be quite confident that you have the right answer. It still won't hurt to check the other answer choices, but most of the time, you've got it!

Answer the Question

It may seem obvious to only pick answer choices that answer the question, but the test writers can create some excellent answer choices that are wrong. Don't pick an answer just because it sounds right, or you believe it to be true. It MUST answer the question. Once you've made your selection, always go back and check it against the question and make sure that you didn't misread the question, and the answer choice does answer the question posed.

Benchmark

After you read the first answer choice, decide if you think it sounds correct or not. If it doesn't, move on to the next answer choice. If it does, mentally mark that answer choice. This doesn't mean that you've definitely selected it as your answer choice, it just means that it's the best you've seen thus far. Go ahead and read the next choice. If the next choice is worse than the one you've already selected, keep going to the next answer choice. If the next choice is better than the choice you've already selected, mentally mark the new answer choice as your best guess.

The first answer choice that you select becomes your standard. Every other answer choice must be benchmarked against that standard. That choice is correct until proven otherwise by another answer choice beating it out. Once you've decided that no other answer choice seems as good, do one final check to ensure that your answer choice answers the question posed.

Valid Information

Don't discount any of the information provided in the question. Every piece of information may be necessary to determine the correct answer. None of the information in the question is there to throw you off (while the answer choices will certainly have information to throw you off). If two seemingly unrelated topics are discussed, don't ignore either. You can be confident there is a relationship, or it wouldn't be included in the question, and you are probably going to have to determine what is that relationship to find the answer.

Avoid "Fact Traps"

Don't get distracted by a choice that is factually true. Your search is for the answer that answers the question. Stay focused and don't fall for an answer that is true but incorrect. Always go back to the question and make sure you're choosing an answer that actually answers the question and is not just a true statement. An answer can be factually correct, but it MUST answer the question asked. Additionally, two answers can both be seemingly correct, so be sure to read all of the answer choices, and make sure that you get the one that BEST answers the question.

Milk the Question

Some of the questions may throw you completely off. They might deal with a subject you have not been exposed to, or one that you haven't reviewed in years. While your lack of knowledge about the subject will be a hindrance, the question itself can give you many clues that will help you find the correct answer. Read the question carefully and look for clues. Watch particularly for adjectives and nouns describing difficult terms or words that you

Copyright © Mometrix Media. You have been licensed one copy of this document for personal use only. Any other reproduction or redistribution is strictly prohibited. All rights reserved.

don't recognize. Regardless of if you completely understand a word or not, replacing it with a synonym either provided or one you more familiar with may help you to understand what the questions are asking. Rather than wracking your mind about specific detailed information concerning a difficult term or word, try to use mental substitutes that are easier to understand.

The Trap of Familiarity

Don't just choose a word because you recognize it. On difficult questions, you may not recognize a number of words in the answer choices. The test writers don't put "make-believe" words on the test; so don't think that just because you only recognize all the words in one answer choice means that answer choice must be correct. If you only recognize words in one answer choice, then focus on that one. Is it correct? Try your best to determine if it is correct. If it is, that is great, but if it doesn't, eliminate it. Each word and answer choice you eliminate increases your chances of getting the question correct, even if you then have to guess among the unfamiliar choices.

Eliminate Answers

Eliminate choices as soon as you realize they are wrong. But be careful! Make sure you consider all of the possible answer choices. Just because one appears right, doesn't mean that the next one won't be even better! The test writers will usually put more than one good answer choice for every question, so read all of them. Don't worry if you are stuck between two that seem right. By getting down to just two remaining possible choices, your odds are now 50/50. Rather than wasting too much time, play the odds. You are guessing, but guessing wisely, because you've been able to knock out some of the answer choices that you know are wrong. If you are eliminating choices and realize that the last answer choice you are left with is also obviously wrong, don't panic. Start over and consider each choice again. There may easily be something that you missed the first time and will realize on the second pass.

Tough Questions

If you are stumped on a problem or it appears too hard or too difficult, don't waste time. Move on! Remember though, if you can quickly check for obviously incorrect answer choices, your chances of guessing correctly are greatly improved. Before you completely give up, at least try to knock out a couple of possible answers. Eliminate what you can and then guess at the remaining answer choices before moving on.

Brainstorm

If you get stuck on a difficult question, spend a few seconds quickly brainstorming. Run through the complete list of possible answer choices. Look at each choice and ask yourself, "Could this answer the question satisfactorily?" Go through each answer choice and consider it independently of the other. By systematically going through all possibilities, you may find something that you would otherwise overlook. Remember that when you get stuck, it's important to try to keep moving.

Read Carefully

Understand the problem. Read the question and answer choices carefully. Don't miss the question because you misread the terms. You have plenty of time to read each question thoroughly and make sure you understand what is being asked. Yet a happy medium must be attained, so don't waste too much time. You must read carefully, but efficiently.

Copyright © Mometrix Media. You have been licensed one copy of this document for personal use only. Any other reproduction or redistribution is strictly prohibited. All rights reserved.

Face Value

When in doubt, use common sense. Always accept the situation in the problem at face value. Don't read too much into it. These problems will not require you to make huge leaps of logic. The test writers aren't trying to throw you off with a cheap trick. If you have to go beyond creativity and make a leap of logic in order to have an answer choice answer the question, then you should look at the other answer choices. Don't overcomplicate the problem by creating theoretical relationships or explanations that will warp time or space. These are normal problems rooted in reality. It's just that the applicable relationship or explanation may not be readily apparent and you have to figure things out. Use your common sense to interpret anything that isn't clear.

Prefixes

If you're having trouble with a word in the question or answer choices, try dissecting it. Take advantage of every clue that the word might include. Prefixes and suffixes can be a huge help. Usually they allow you to determine a basic meaning. Pre- means before, post- means after, pro - is positive, de- is negative. From these prefixes and suffixes, you can get an idea of the general meaning of the word and try to put it into context. Beware though of any traps. Just because con is the opposite of pro, doesn't necessarily mean congress is the opposite of progress!

Hedge Phrases

Watch out for critical "hedge" phrases, such as likely, may, can, will often, sometimes, often, almost, mostly, usually, generally, rarely, sometimes. Question writers insert these hedge phrases to cover every possibility. Often an answer choice will be wrong simply because it leaves no room for exception. Avoid answer choices that have definitive words like "exactly," and "always".

Switchback Words

Stay alert for "switchbacks". These are the words and phrases frequently used to alert you to shifts in thought. The most common switchback word is "but". Others include although, however, nevertheless, on the other hand, even though, while, in spite of, despite, regardless of.

New Information

Correct answer choices will rarely have completely new information included. Answer choices typically are straightforward reflections of the material asked about and will directly relate to the question. If a new piece of information is included in an answer choice that doesn't even seem to relate to the topic being asked about, then that answer choice is likely incorrect. All of the information needed to answer the question is usually provided for you, and so you should not have to make guesses that are unsupported or choose answer choices that require unknown information that cannot be reasoned on its own.

Time Management

On technical questions, don't get lost on the technical terms. Don't spend too much time on any one question. If you don't know what a term means, then since you don't have a dictionary, odds are you aren't going to get much further. You should immediately recognize terms as whether or not you know them. If you don't, work with the other clues that you have, the other answer choices and terms provided, but don't waste too much time trying to figure out a difficult term.

Copyright © Mometrix Media. You have been licensed one copy of this document for personal use only. Any other reproduction or redistribution is strictly prohibited. All rights reserved.

Contextual Clues

Look for contextual clues. An answer can be right but not correct. The contextual clues will help you find the answer that is most right and is correct. Understand the context in which a phrase or statement is made. This will help you make important distinctions.

Don't Panic

Panicking will not answer any questions for you. Therefore, it isn't helpful. When you first see the question, if your mind goes blank, take a deep breath. Force yourself to mechanically go through the steps of solving the problem and using the strategies you've learned.

Pace Yourself

Don't get clock fever. It's easy to be overwhelmed when you're looking at a page full of questions, your mind is full of random thoughts and feeling confused, and the clock is ticking down faster than you would like. Calm down and maintain the pace that you have set for yourself. As long as you are on track by monitoring your pace, you are guaranteed to have enough time for yourself. When you get to the last few minutes of the test, it may seem like you won't have enough time left, but if you only have as many questions as you should have left at that point, then you're right on track!

Answer Selection

The best way to pick an answer choice is to eliminate all of those that are wrong, until only one is left and confirm that is the correct answer. Sometimes though, an answer choice may immediately look right. Be careful! Take a second to make sure that the other choices are not equally obvious. Don't make a hasty mistake. There are only two times that you should stop before checking other answers. First is when you are positive that the answer choice you have selected is correct. Second is when time is almost out and you have to make a quick guess!

Check Your Work

Since you will probably not know every term listed and the answer to every question, it is important that you get credit for the ones that you do know. Don't miss any questions through careless mistakes. If at all possible, try to take a second to look back over your answer selection and make sure you've selected the correct answer choice and haven't made a costly careless mistake (such as marking an answer choice that you didn't mean to mark). This quick double check should more than pay for itself in caught mistakes for the time it costs.

Beware of Directly Quoted Answers

Sometimes an answer choice will repeat word for word a portion of the question or reference section. However, beware of such exact duplication – it may be a trap! More than likely, the correct choice will paraphrase or summarize a point, rather than being exactly the same wording.

Slang

Scientific sounding answers are better than slang ones. An answer choice that begins "To compare the outcomes..." is much more likely to be correct than one that begins "Because some people insisted..."

Copyright © Mometrix Media. You have been licensed one copy of this document for personal use only. Any other reproduction or redistribution is strictly prohibited. All rights reserved.

Extreme Statements

Avoid wild answers that throw out highly controversial ideas that are proclaimed as established fact. An answer choice that states the "process should be used in certain situations, if..." is much more likely to be correct than one that states the "process should be discontinued completely." The first is a calm rational statement and doesn't even make a definitive, uncompromising stance, using a hedge word "if" to provide wiggle room, whereas the second choice is a radical idea and far more extreme.

Answer Choice Families

When you have two or more answer choices that are direct opposites or parallels, one of them is usually the correct answer. For instance, if one answer choice states "x increases" and another answer choice states "x decreases" or "y increases," then those two or three answer choices are very similar in construction and fall into the same family of answer choices. A family of answer choices is when two or three answer choices are very similar in construction, and yet often have a directly opposite meaning. Usually the correct answer choice will be in that family of answer choices. The "odd man out" or answer choice that doesn't seem to fit the parallel construction of the other answer choices is more likely to be incorrect.

Copyright © Mometrix Media. You have been licensed one copy of this document for personal use only. Any other reproduction or redistribution is strictly prohibited. All rights reserved.

Special Report: How to Overcome Test Anxiety

The very nature of tests caters to some level of anxiety, nervousness or tension, just as we feel for any important event that occurs in our lives. A little bit of anxiety or nervousness can be a good thing. It helps us with motivation, and makes achievement just that much sweeter. However, too much anxiety can be a problem; especially if it hinders our ability to function and perform.

"Test anxiety," is the term that refers to the emotional reactions that some test-takers experience when faced with a test or exam. Having a fear of testing and exams is based upon a rational fear, since the test-taker's performance can shape the course of an academic career. Nevertheless, experiencing excessive fear of examinations will only interfere with the test-takers ability to perform, and his/her chances to be successful.

There are a large variety of causes that can contribute to the development and sensation of test anxiety. These include, but are not limited to lack of performance and worrying about issues surrounding the test.

Lack of Preparation

Lack of preparation can be identified by the following behaviors or situations:

Not scheduling enough time to study, and therefore cramming the night before the test or exam
Managing time poorly, to create the sensation that there is not enough time to do everything
Failing to organize the text information in advance, so that the study material consists of the entire text and not simply the pertinent information
Poor overall studying habits

Worrying, on the other hand, can be related to both the test taker, or many other factors around him/her that will be affected by the results of the test. These include worrying about:

Previous performances on similar exams, or exams in general
How friends and other students are achieving
The negative consequences that will result from a poor grade or failure

There are three primary elements to test anxiety. Physical components, which involve the same typical bodily reactions as those to acute anxiety (to be discussed below). Emotional factors have to do with fear or panic. Mental or cognitive issues concerning attention spans and memory abilities.

Copyright © Mometrix Media. You have been licensed one copy of this document for personal use only. Any other reproduction or redistribution is strictly prohibited. All rights reserved.

Physical Signals

There are many different symptoms of test anxiety, and these are not limited to mental and emotional strain. Frequently there are a range of physical signals that will let a test taker know that he/she is suffering from test anxiety. These bodily changes can include the following:

Perspiring
Sweaty palms
Wet, trembling hands
Nausea
Dry mouth
A knot in the stomach
Headache
Faintness
Muscle tension
Aching shoulders, back and neck
Rapid heart beat
Feeling too hot/cold

To recognize the sensation of test anxiety, a test-taker should monitor him/herself for the following sensations:

The physical distress symptoms as listed above
Emotional sensitivity, expressing emotional feelings such as the need to cry or laugh too much, or a sensation of anger or helplessness
A decreased ability to think, causing the test-taker to blank out or have racing thoughts that are hard to organize or control.

Though most students will feel some level of anxiety when faced with a test or exam, the majority can cope with that anxiety and maintain it at a manageable level. However, those who cannot are faced with a very real and very serious condition, which can and should be controlled for the immeasurable benefit of this sufferer.

Naturally, these sensations lead to negative results for the testing experience. The most common effects of test anxiety have to do with nervousness and mental blocking.

Nervousness

Nervousness can appear in several different levels:

The test-taker's difficulty, or even inability to read and understand the questions on the test
The difficulty or inability to organize thoughts to a coherent form
The difficulty or inability to recall key words and concepts relating to the testing questions (especially essays)
The receipt of poor grades on a test, though the test material was well known by the test taker

Copyright © Mometrix Media. You have been licensed one copy of this document for personal use only. Any other reproduction or redistribution is strictly prohibited. All rights reserved.

Conversely, a person may also experience mental blocking, which involves:

Blanking out on test questions
Only remembering the correct answers to the questions when the test has already finished.

Fortunately for test anxiety sufferers, beating these feelings, to a large degree, has to do with proper preparation. When a test taker has a feeling of preparedness, then anxiety will be dramatically lessened.

The first step to resolving anxiety issues is to distinguish which of the two types of anxiety are being suffered. If the anxiety is a direct result of a lack of preparation, this should be considered a normal reaction, and the anxiety level (as opposed to the test results) shouldn't be anything to worry about. However, if, when adequately prepared, the test-taker still panics, blanks out, or seems to overreact, this is not a fully rational reaction. While this can be considered normal too, there are many ways to combat and overcome these effects.

Remember that anxiety cannot be entirely eliminated, however, there are ways to minimize it, to make the anxiety easier to manage. Preparation is one of the best ways to minimize test anxiety. Therefore the following techniques are wise in order to best fight off any anxiety that may want to build.

To begin with, try to avoid cramming before a test, whenever it is possible. By trying to memorize an entire term's worth of information in one day, you'll be shocking your system, and not giving yourself a very good chance to absorb the information. This is an easy path to anxiety, so for those who suffer from test anxiety, cramming should not even be considered an option.

Instead of cramming, work throughout the semester to combine all of the material which is presented throughout the semester, and work on it gradually as the course goes by, making sure to master the main concepts first, leaving minor details for a week or so before the test.

To study for the upcoming exam, be sure to pose questions that may be on the examination, to gauge the ability to answer them by integrating the ideas from your texts, notes and lectures, as well as any supplementary readings.

If it is truly impossible to cover all of the information that was covered in that particular term, concentrate on the most important portions, that can be covered very well. Learn these concepts as best as possible, so that when the test comes, a goal can be made to use these concepts as presentations of your knowledge.

In addition to study habits, changes in attitude are critical to beating a struggle with test anxiety. In fact, an improvement of the perspective over the entire test-taking experience can actually help a test taker to enjoy studying and therefore improve the overall experience. Be certain not to overemphasize the significance of the grade - know that the result of the test is neither a reflection of self worth, nor is it a measure of intelligence; one grade will not predict a person's future success.

Copyright © Mometrix Media. You have been licensed one copy of this document for personal use only. Any other reproduction or redistribution is strictly prohibited. All rights reserved.

To improve an overall testing outlook, the following steps should be tried:

Keeping in mind that the most reasonable expectation for taking a test is to expect to try to demonstrate as much of what you know as you possibly can.
Reminding ourselves that a test is only one test; this is not the only one, and there will be others.
The thought of thinking of oneself in an irrational, all-or-nothing term should be avoided at all costs.
A reward should be designated for after the test, so there's something to look forward to. Whether it be going to a movie, going out to eat, or simply visiting friends, schedule it in advance, and do it no matter what result is expected on the exam.

Test-takers should also keep in mind that the basics are some of the most important things, even beyond anti-anxiety techniques and studying. Never neglect the basic social, emotional and biological needs, in order to try to absorb information. In order to best achieve, these three factors must be held as just as important as the studying itself.

Study Steps

Remember the following important steps for studying:

Maintain healthy nutrition and exercise habits. Continue both your recreational activities and social pass times. These both contribute to your physical and emotional well being.
Be certain to get a good amount of sleep, especially the night before the test, because when you're overtired you are not able to perform to the best of your best ability.
Keep the studying pace to a moderate level by taking breaks when they are needed, and varying the work whenever possible, to keep the mind fresh instead of getting bored. When enough studying has been done that all the material that can be learned has been learned, and the test taker is prepared for the test, stop studying and do something relaxing such as listening to music, watching a movie, or taking a warm bubble bath.

There are also many other techniques to minimize the uneasiness or apprehension that is experienced along with test anxiety before, during, or even after the examination. In fact, there are a great deal of things that can be done to stop anxiety from interfering with lifestyle and performance. Again, remember that anxiety will not be eliminated entirely, and it shouldn't be. Otherwise that "up" feeling for exams would not exist, and most of us depend on that sensation to perform better than usual. However, this anxiety has to be at a level that is manageable.

Of course, as we have just discussed, being prepared for the exam is half the battle right away. Attending all classes, finding out what knowledge will be expected on the exam, and knowing the exam schedules are easy steps to lowering anxiety. Keeping up with work will remove the need to cram, and efficient study habits will eliminate wasted time. Studying should be done in an ideal location for concentration, so that it is simple to become interested in the material and give it complete attention. A method such as SQ3R (Survey, Question, Read, Recite, Review) is a wonderful key to follow to make sure that the study habits are as effective as possible, especially in the case of learning from a

Copyright © Mometrix Media. You have been licensed one copy of this document for personal use only. Any other reproduction or redistribution is strictly prohibited. All rights reserved.

textbook. Flashcards are great techniques for memorization. Learning to take good notes will mean that notes will be full of useful information, so that less sifting will need to be done to seek out what is pertinent for studying. Reviewing notes after class and then again on occasion will keep the information fresh in the mind. From notes that have been taken summary sheets and outlines can be made for simpler reviewing.

A study group can also be a very motivational and helpful place to study, as there will be a sharing of ideas, all of the minds can work together, to make sure that everyone understands, and the studying will be made more interesting because it will be a social occasion.

Basically, though, as long as the test-taker remains organized and self confident, with efficient study habits, less time will need to be spent studying, and higher grades will be achieved.

To become self confident, there are many useful steps. The first of these is "self talk." It has been shown through extensive research, that self-talk for students who suffer from test anxiety, should be well monitored, in order to make sure that it contributes to self confidence as opposed to sinking the student. Frequently the self talk of test-anxious students is negative or self-defeating, thinking that everyone else is smarter and faster, that they always mess up, and that if they don't do well, they'll fail the entire course. It is important to decreasing anxiety that awareness is made of self talk. Try writing any negative self thoughts and then disputing them with a positive statement instead. Begin self-encouragement as though it was a friend speaking. Repeat positive statements to help reprogram the mind to believing in successes instead of failures.

Helpful Techniques

Other extremely helpful techniques include:

Self-visualization of doing well and reaching goals
While aiming for an "A" level of understanding, don't try to "overprotect" by setting your expectations lower. This will only convince the mind to stop studying in order to meet the lower expectations.
Don't make comparisons with the results or habits of other students. These are individual factors, and different things work for different people, causing different results.
Strive to become an expert in learning what works well, and what can be done in order to improve. Consider collecting this data in a journal.
Create rewards for after studying instead of doing things before studying that will only turn into avoidance behaviors.
Make a practice of relaxing - by using methods such as progressive relaxation, self-hypnosis, guided imagery, etc - in order to make relaxation an automatic sensation.
Work on creating a state of relaxed concentration so that concentrating will take on the focus of the mind, so that none will be wasted on worrying.
Take good care of the physical self by eating well and getting enough sleep.
Plan in time for exercise and stick to this plan.

Copyright © Mometrix Media. You have been licensed one copy of this document for personal use only. Any other reproduction or redistribution is strictly prohibited. All rights reserved.

Beyond these techniques, there are other methods to be used before, during and after the test that will help the test-taker perform well in addition to overcoming anxiety. Before the exam comes the academic preparation. This involves establishing a study schedule and beginning at least one week before the actual date of the test. By doing this, the anxiety of not having enough time to study for the test will be automatically eliminated. Moreover, this will make the studying a much more effective experience, ensuring that the learning will be an easier process. This relieves much undue pressure on the test-taker.

Summary sheets, note cards, and flash cards with the main concepts and examples of these main concepts should be prepared in advance of the actual studying time. A topic should never be eliminated from this process. By omitting a topic because it isn't expected to be on the test is only setting up the test-taker for anxiety should it actually appear on the exam. Utilize the course syllabus for laying out the topics that should be studied. Carefully go over the notes that were made in class, paying special attention to any of the issues that the professor took special care to emphasize while lecturing in class. In the textbooks, use the chapter review, or if possible, the chapter tests, to begin your review.

It may even be possible to ask the instructor what information will be covered on the exam, or what the format of the exam will be (for example, multiple choice, essay, free form, true-false). Additionally, see if it is possible to find out how many questions will be on the test. If a review sheet or sample test has been offered by the professor, make good use of it, above anything else, for the preparation for the test. Another great resource for getting to know the examination is reviewing tests from previous semesters. Use these tests to review, and aim to achieve a 100% score on each of the possible topics. With a few exceptions, the goal that you set for yourself is the highest one that you will reach.

Take all of the questions that were assigned as homework, and rework them to any other possible course material. The more problems reworked, the more skill and confidence will form as a result. When forming the solution to a problem, write out each of the steps. Don't simply do head work. By doing as many steps on paper as possible, much clarification and therefore confidence will be formed. Do this with as many homework problems as possible, before checking the answers. By checking the answer after each problem, a reinforcement will exist, that will not be on the exam. Study situations should be as exam-like as possible, to prime the test-taker's system for the experience. By waiting to check the answers at the end, a psychological advantage will be formed, to decrease the stress factor.

Another fantastic reason for not cramming is the avoidance of confusion in concepts, especially when it comes to mathematics. 8-10 hours of study will become one hundred percent more effective if it is spread out over a week or at least several days, instead of doing it all in one sitting. Recognize that the human brain requires time in order to assimilate new material, so frequent breaks and a span of study time over several days will be much more beneficial.

Additionally, don't study right up until the point of the exam. Studying should stop a minimum of one hour before the exam begins. This allows the brain to rest and put things in their proper order. This will also provide the time to become as relaxed as

Copyright © Mometrix Media. You have been licensed one copy of this document for personal use only. Any other reproduction or redistribution is strictly prohibited. All rights reserved.

possible when going into the examination room. The test-taker will also have time to eat well and eat sensibly. Know that the brain needs food as much as the rest of the body. With enough food and enough sleep, as well as a relaxed attitude, the body and the mind are primed for success.

Avoid any anxious classmates who are talking about the exam. These students only spread anxiety, and are not worth sharing the anxious sentimentalities.

Before the test also involves creating a positive attitude, so mental preparation should also be a point of concentration. There are many keys to creating a positive attitude. Should fears become rushing in, make a visualization of taking the exam, doing well, and seeing an A written on the paper. Write out a list of affirmations that will bring a feeling of confidence, such as "I am doing well in my English class," "I studied well and know my material," "I enjoy this class." Even if the affirmations aren't believed at first, it sends a positive message to the subconscious which will result in an alteration of the overall belief system, which is the system that creates reality.

If a sensation of panic begins, work with the fear and imagine the very worst! Work through the entire scenario of not passing the test, failing the entire course, and dropping out of school, followed by not getting a job, and pushing a shopping cart through the dark alley where you'll live. This will place things into perspective! Then, practice deep breathing and create a visualization of the opposite situation - achieving an "A" on the exam, passing the entire course, receiving the degree at a graduation ceremony.

On the day of the test, there are many things to be done to ensure the best results, as well as the most calm outlook. The following stages are suggested in order to maximize test-taking potential:

Begin the examination day with a moderate breakfast, and avoid any coffee or beverages with caffeine if the test taker is prone to jitters. Even people who are used to managing caffeine can feel jittery or light-headed when it is taken on a test day.
Attempt to do something that is relaxing before the examination begins. As last minute cramming clouds the mastering of overall concepts, it is better to use this time to create a calming outlook.
Be certain to arrive at the test location well in advance, in order to provide time to select a location that is away from doors, windows and other distractions, as well as giving enough time to relax before the test begins.
Keep away from anxiety generating classmates who will upset the sensation of stability and relaxation that is being attempted before the exam.
Should the waiting period before the exam begins cause anxiety, create a self-distraction by reading a light magazine or something else that is relaxing and simple.

During the exam itself, read the entire exam from beginning to end, and find out how much time should be allotted to each individual problem. Once writing the exam, should more time be taken for a problem, it should be abandoned, in order to begin another problem. If there is time at the end, the unfinished problem can always be returned to and completed.

Copyright © Mometrix Media. You have been licensed one copy of this document for personal use only. Any other reproduction or redistribution is strictly prohibited. All rights reserved.

Read the instructions very carefully - twice - so that unpleasant surprises won't follow during or after the exam has ended.

When writing the exam, pretend that the situation is actually simply the completion of homework within a library, or at home. This will assist in forming a relaxed atmosphere, and will allow the brain extra focus for the complex thinking function.

Begin the exam with all of the questions with which the most confidence is felt. This will build the confidence level regarding the entire exam and will begin a quality momentum. This will also create encouragement for trying the problems where uncertainty resides.

Going with the "gut instinct" is always the way to go when solving a problem. Second guessing should be avoided at all costs. Have confidence in the ability to do well.

For essay questions, create an outline in advance that will keep the mind organized and make certain that all of the points are remembered. For multiple choice, read every answer, even if the correct one has been spotted - a better one may exist.

Continue at a pace that is reasonable and not rushed, in order to be able to work carefully. Provide enough time to go over the answers at the end, to check for small errors that can be corrected.

Should a feeling of panic begin, breathe deeply, and think of the feeling of the body releasing sand through its pores. Visualize a calm, peaceful place, and include all of the sights, sounds and sensations of this image. Continue the deep breathing, and take a few minutes to continue this with closed eyes. When all is well again, return to the test.

If a "blanking" occurs for a certain question, skip it and move on to the next question. There will be time to return to the other question later. Get everything done that can be done, first, to guarantee all the grades that can be compiled, and to build all of the confidence possible. Then return to the weaker questions to build the marks from there.

Remember, one's own reality can be created, so as long as the belief is there, success will follow. And remember: anxiety can happen later, right now, there's an exam to be written!

After the examination is complete, whether there is a feeling for a good grade or a bad grade, don't dwell on the exam, and be certain to follow through on the reward that was promised...and enjoy it! Don't dwell on any mistakes that have been made, as there is nothing that can be done at this point anyway.

Additionally, don't begin to study for the next test right away. Do something relaxing for a while, and let the mind relax and prepare itself to begin absorbing information again.

From the results of the exam - both the grade and the entire experience, be certain to learn from what has gone on. Perfect studying habits and work some more on confidence in order to make the next examination experience even better than the last one.

Copyright © Mometrix Media. You have been licensed one copy of this document for personal use only. Any other reproduction or redistribution is strictly prohibited. All rights reserved.

Learn to avoid places where openings occurred for laziness, procrastination and day dreaming.

Use the time between this exam and the next one to better learn to relax, even learning to relax on cue, so that any anxiety can be controlled during the next exam. Learn how to relax the body. Slouch in your chair if that helps. Tighten and then relax all of the different muscle groups, one group at a time, beginning with the feet and then working all the way up to the neck and face. This will ultimately relax the muscles more than they were to begin with. Learn how to breathe deeply and comfortably, and focus on this breathing going in and out as a relaxing thought. With every exhale, repeat the word "relax."

As common as test anxiety is, it is very possible to overcome it. Make yourself one of the test-takers who overcome this frustrating hindrance.

Copyright © Mometrix Media. You have been licensed one copy of this document for personal use only. Any other reproduction or redistribution is strictly prohibited. All rights reserved.

Special Report: Additional Bonus Material

Due to our efforts to try to keep this book to a manageable length, we've created a link that will give you access to all of your additional bonus material.

Please visit http://www.mometrix.com/bonus948/gacephysics to access the information.

Copyright © Mometrix Media. You have been licensed one copy of this document for personal use only. Any other reproduction or redistribution is strictly prohibited. All rights reserved.